ULTIMATE BENCH WARRIOR

How to Design, Build, and Modify Custom Guitar and Bass Amplifiers

By Lee Jackson

Cover art by Levin Pfeufer

Cherry Lane Music Company
Educational Director/Project Supervisor: Susan Poliniak
Director of Publications: Mark Phillips
Publications Coordinator: Rebecca Skidmore
Editorial Assistant: Natalie Chomet

ISBN 978-1-57560-445-9

Also available from Cherry Lane:
Complete Schematics:
Instrument Amplifier and Effects Schematics
by Lee Jackson
(02500369)

Visit our website at www.cherrylaneprint.com

TABLE OF CONTENTS

ACKNOWLEDGMENTS

I'd first like to start by thanking all of the musicians who allowed me to use their equipment as my palette to create my electronic sounds. I would like to thank Phil Brown for his help and for being a great friend, and Randy Kemper for helping me with my commas, periods, and dotting my "i's". I would like to thank all of the employees who currently work with me and have worked for me in the past, who have contributed to the overall sound and quality of my products. Thanks to Pignose, Rivera Research, Oberhiem, B.C. Rich, Fender, Ampeg, and Crate for allowing me to work for them. And thanks to my own companies Metaltronix, Perfect Connection, and Lee Jackson Amplifiers.

This book is dedicated to all of the amp designers who have felt that good was not good enough.

Lee Jackson

FOREWORD

The first time I heard of Lee Jackson, I was at some very high-tech rehearsal studio getting ready to do an album for a major recording artist. The sound I was getting was good, but something was missing. I couldn't put my finger on it. I'm from the old school—just plug straight into the amp and blow.

Fortunately, during a break I chanced upon a bulletin board, and tucked way off in the corner was a piece of paper with a name and number. "Lee Jackson Amp Doctor. Want that sound? Then call me. Reasonable rates." or some such thing.

You see, Mr. Jackson had a serious underground reputation. Metal was going full bore and I was a guitarist/singer-songwriter trying everything under the sun to connect with the real deal. I called that number and asked for an address. For some reason I took my old Marshall and Hiwatt over and met this guy who was taller than I was, with jeans, boots, and long hair—and somehow I just knew that we were going to do something special to my gear. He asked me to plug into one of his amplifiers there at his shop. I think I played for several minutes. I put my guitar down and said to Lee, "Well, they're yours! Make them love me again!"

Three days later I picked them up and went to the studio and made some fat money, and everybody raved about the great sound. I have an opinion about guitar players as a rule: We're like old gunfighters who can play the fastest and the loudest. Fortune smiled upon me when Lee helped recapture the magical sound that was missing, and I was able to translate the essence of the creative spirit in my music, and for many other artists who I have worked with.

The day that I met Lee was a turning point for me. He became one of my very best and dearest friends. There is something about this genius that makes me feel good about myself and my environment, both personally and professionally. Lee is able to transcend the limitations of the mass consumer market, and in a world full of ne'er-do-wells and wanna-bes, Lee's the real deal.

This book that you're reading is not just for anybody. It's for those of you who love to tinker and create beyond the bounds of "safe and normal" reality, and who move to the sound of a different drummer. I thank God that I met Lee. This information has been culled from thousands and thousands of hours spent designing and sweating over circuit boards and solder, and from building and marketing amplifiers around the world.

Do you want to know something? You can now build your dream sound and have fun knowing that the next power chord is going to wake up the neighborhood, and will turn you into a wonderful technician/player/musical avatar.

Life is good, isn't it? By the way, "good" just got a whole lot better. Lee Jackson, we are all far more than we would have allowed ourselves to be, and I thank you for it. Hey! Everybody check this out and build it, and then go blow your mind. Believe me—it's a beautiful thing.

Shemhamephorae,
Phil Brown

INTRODUCTION

I have always been interested in doing experiments on electronic equipment of all kinds. I was brought up in an environment of music and electronics. My father owned a shop that had a record store in the front and an electronic repair shop in the back. I have often wondered how I was influenced by my upbringing. I was told that my mother was working in the record shop the whole time she was pregnant with me. The music store was always rocking with the sounds of the '60s, and because my father was into electronics, it was only natural for me to follow in his footsteps. Even with my earliest guitar equipment, I couldn't leave it alone. My first amplifier was a record player with a single 12-inch speaker in the lid—the kind that you would find in old school houses. These had a mic input that I would plug my guitar into. Because these old players had tubes, they sounded great if you turned them all the way up. I started tinkering and modifying the player by adding more gain; I also learned to respect the high voltages of tube amps. It takes only a few instances of touching those high voltages to figure out how much it *really* hurts. As my playing progressed, so did my need for more power. I moved on to Fender Twins and Marshall 100-watt heads, finding that the stock equipment didn't give me the sound I was looking for. So, on went my quest for the perfect tone, and the only way of getting it was to experiment. When I first started working on my amps, the latest breakthrough was a master volume. I remember meeting one of the designers of the Standell amplifiers, and he showed me his latest discovery, the "master volume." I thought it was great and rushed home to tear apart my Marshall to install it. Well, this fanned the fire because even with the master volume it still needed more gain! So I started experimenting with adding gain stages in different places of the circuit and seeing how it affected the sound. It makes a big difference where you place the different stages and how much gain you add to each stage. Each person hears sound differently, so it is important to experiment to get something to sound good to *you*. If you are doing this professionally, hopefully the sound you like will be appealing to others, too.

When I was writing this book, I was thinking that I wished that there was a book like this available when I started. I could have used it as a reference while I was experimenting on my amplifiers. You will find that most amplifier companies take ideas from other amplifiers that they have seen. When I went to work for Ampeg, I found files on my companies and me with notes on the features they liked. Each company checks out what the other companies are doing, and then they take those ideas and try to improve upon them—that's why I included schematics from other companies. Not only are they good for repairing your older amps, they are also good for seeing what others have done so that you have some designs to start with when you are creating your new sound.

In this book, I cover the basics of soldering, which is very important if you want an amplifier to work past the first time you accidentally drop it. I also cover the basic tools of the trade (the equipment you will need to build your dream amp), different tube types, and a little history of tubes and tube manufacturing. I show some solid-state circuits, like buffers and splitters, power supplies, and mixers. There's a section on amplifier modifications, which covers everything from gain stages to adding reverbs, and shows modifications to Fenders and Marshalls. I didn't want to make this a textbook, but I threw in enough information to help you with achieving your sound.

Always, remember to be *very careful.* Tube amplifiers are the best, but ***they can kill you!*** So use extreme caution when working with and on them.

Have fun—because that's what we are here for—and remember to experiment. There are no specific ways in which to design amplifiers. The best amplifiers on the market all exist because someone wanted a better sound and took the time to experiment with different possibilities. Several of my friends expressed concern for me showing some of my design ideas to the public. I feel that there is plenty of room at the top because the bottom is full. So have fun with your next adventure.

Lee Jackson in his design shop

You can reach Lee through his website at http://www.leejackson.com.

Safety Warning and Disclaimer

Tube Amplifiers contain high voltages that can be lethal, even if the amplifier has been "off" for some time. I do NOT recommend that you open an amplifier or try to perform any repair or modification operations unless you are properly trained in electronic servicing. Lee Jackson and/or his affiliates accept NO responsibility for accidents resulting in personal injury, death, or destruction of property. There are VERY large voltages present in your amplifier that can kill, even with the amplifier unplugged from the wall.

IF YOU HAVE ANY QUESTION IN YOUR MIND AS TO WHETHER YOU CAN DO ANY OF THIS WORK SAFELY, THEN YOU CAN'T! SEEK EXPERIENCED HELP!

Trademarks

All of the terms mentioned in this book that are known to be trademarks and/or brand names are listed below. Lee Jackson is not affiliated or a manufacturer of any of these products: Acoustical Manufacturing Co. (now QUAD Electroacoustics Ltd.), Ampeg, Bedrock, Bell Labs, Boss, Celestion, Crate, Fender, General Electric, Gibson, Groove Tubes, Hiwatt, International Music Corporation, Laney, Marshall, Mesa/Boogie, Music Man, Neutrik, Orange, Peavey, Pignose, Roland, Seymour Duncan, Sears Silvertone, Soldano, Sound City, Sovtek, Standel, Traynor, Vox, and Yamaha Corporation of America

CHAPTER 1
TOOLS OF THE TRADE

Tools

In this section, I'll talk about some of the larger tools that you will need to service your amplifiers. I won't cover small hand tools (screwdrivers, pliers, wrenches, etc.) because those are things that you should have anyway. But I will cover some of the chemicals that I like to use, such as cleaners, lubricants, and so forth; these things are not mandatory, but they may make your life a lot easier.

Greenlee Punches

These are necessities when you are putting holes in an amplifier chassis. They are well worth what they cost, and they last forever.

To use a greenlee punch, first drill a 3/8" hole. Next, insert one half of the punch on each side, and then tighten this with a wrench until the halves of the punch meet. This will make a very clean hole in a reasonably short amount of time, as opposed to using a file, which takes a very long time. Greenlee punches come in various sizes that can accommodate just about any hole size. The very large punches require a 1/2" drill hole.

Heat Guns

There are many different heat guns out there, but I prefer the larger ones. Heat guns are great for working with heat shrink tubing and for baking the moisture out of old Fender fiber circuitboards. When these fibreboards get old, they suck up moisture and start to conduct across the circuit eyelets. This can cause an amp to crackle and pop, and sometimes lack gain. This can be fixed by using a gun to heat up the fiber circuitboard until the wax that is impregnated starts to bubble—but the absolute best solution is to take out all of the parts and bake the board in an oven.

Scopes

For all signal testing, the oscilloscope is by far the most important instrument on the bench. This scope will not only show you the peak-to-peak voltage of a signal, but it will also show you its waveform. In addition, it can show you the location and cause of distortion in a circuit, as any change in its signal waveform means distortion of the output. Unequal amplification of both halves of a wave, clipping, and many other problems can be found quickly with a scope.

With only two tests, you can tell whether a given stage is passing a signal or amplifying it as much as it should. You can locate dead stages by signal tracing. To do this, touch the scope probe to the input; then, touch it to the output of the stage and notice any difference. If you have signal at the input but none at the output, the stage is dead.

The scope can also perform one test that nothing else can: With a touch of the scope probe on the filter capacitors of an amp's power supply, you can locate the cause of hum, signal feedback, and oscillation.

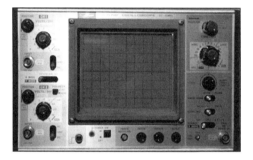

Signal Generators

You will need a unit that produces a test signal to plug into the input of your amplifier. To do this, you need a signal generator—also called a *sine wave generator*. These generators control the frequency and amplitude of a signal; they typically cover a range from 20 Hz to 20 KHz and have a 4- to 5-V (volt) output. For sensitive inputs, you will need the generator to be variable down to 50 mV (millivolts). You don't have to purchase the most expensive generator out there—you just need to make sure that the output has less than three percent distortion on its output.

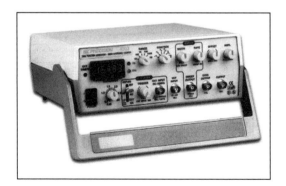

Speaker Loads ("Dummy Loads")

You will need a speaker load to test your amplifier, and particularly when testing tube amplifiers, since tube amps *must* have a speaker load. I use Dale resistors for mine. They range from 10- to 300-watt power-handling capacity. You can get the resistors in various levels so that you can match the impedance of your amplifier.

Here is a circuit for a load resistor with a resistor divider to the BNC connector. This allows you to connect a scope directly to the output stage of an amplifier.

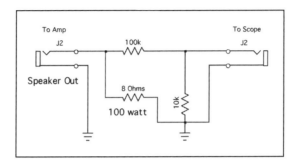

Soldering Guns

These are great for soldering speaker terminals, as well as for soldering anything to an amplifier chassis, as a lot of heat is needed in that case. Soldering guns such as the one shown below are not susceptible to the magnetics of speakers as are soldering stations are, so you don't have to worry about melting the iron. Just don't use these irons to solder small components!

Soldering Stations

Soldering stations are great because they have a variable tip temperature; this allows you to solder anything from the smallest surface-mount component to the back of a control pot. I strongly suggest that you never use these for soldering speakers because the magnetic field of the speaker will magnetize the soldering iron, causing it to go into "thermal runaway" and melt the iron. You can get multiple tips with varying sizes and shapes; I have found that the medium-sized points work best. Soldering stations are not cheap, but I feel that they are well worth their cost.

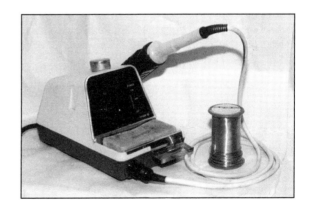

Voltmeters

You will need a meter to read AC and DC voltages. I suggest using a digital voltmeter, since the output is much easier to read than on an analog model. You may see a voltmeter called a *VOM* (for *volt ohm meter*), because nearly all voltmeters also check resistance. Many of these meters also contain AC and DC current meters that can range from a few milliamperes to several amperes. You are limited only by how much you want to or are able to spend.

Variacs

This is a variable-output AC supply transformer. You can adjust the AC line voltage to the amplifier to any level from 0 to 150 VAC. The variac will be your best friend when you are testing amplifier circuits, and with the addition of an amp meter, you can see if a circuit has a short in it without blowing it up first. After a couple of repair jobs, a variac will comfortably pay for itself.

Here is a test fixture that uses a variac with a voltmeter and an amp meter. Be sure to put the fuses in line to protect you and your equipment!

You may have seen articles over the years that describe situations where musicians have used variacs to change the voltage to their amplifiers. However, if you do this but do nothing to your amplifier to compensate for the voltage changes, you will have *big problems!* First of all, if you increase the AC voltage, it increases the voltage not only to the main power supply but to the filament as well. Increased filament voltage means extremely short tube life without any changes in sound. Second of all, if the power supply capacitors' power-handling capacity is not increased to compensate for the increased voltage, these capacitors will explode, leaving little bits of filter cap shrapnel throughout your amplifier. Finally, if you decrease the AC voltage, the filament supply will drop below what it needs to heat the tubes, so the tubes will not turn on at all.

All of that said, there *is* a way to get all of the benefits of this sort of setup without the problems. First, you will need to install another filament transformer, and it will need to be hooked up to the AC line voltage before the variac, or it will need its own AC cord. Second, you will need to increase the filter capacitors' handling voltages. I would get the highest rated voltage at the same capacitance. With these changes, you can comfortably vary the AC line voltage without worries.

Variac Test Stations

Here is a layout for a test station. I would add a double pole, double throw (DPDT) switch before the AC receptacle so you can turn off both sides of the AC line to the amplifier.

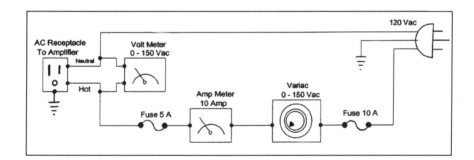

Chemicals

As you've probably heard before, life is better through chemistry. Well, here is a selection of chemicals that I use to clean, lubricate, and glue amplifiers to happiness.

Chiller

Chiller is great when you want to test a part that is working intermittently. You can give the part a blast and see if it acts up or makes noise. You can also cool down output transistors if they are going into thermal runaway.

Corona Dope

You can find this at electronic part shops or television repair shops. Corona Dope is great for fixing a tube socket that you don't have the time to replace. It has the consistency of tar, and it comes with its own applicator. When you have an output tube socket that has arced with carbon across the socket pins, scrape off as much of the carbon as you can and then apply corona dope between the pins and allow it to dry. This will keep the socket from arcing again.

DeoxIT (D5)

This is one of the best cleaners/preservatives on the market. Nearly every studio in the world has seen the benefits of DeoxIT. It is great for control pots, instrument cords, effects pedals, etc. It's a must-have in your arsenal.

Silicon (Glue)

There is no specific brand of silicon that I prefer to use. It is a lot cheaper if you buy it in tubes instead of aerosol cans. Silicon glue is great for holding parts and wires in place and guarding against vibrations that can cause parts to break loose. Do not get silicon glue on solder joints! The vinegar in the glue will cause the solder to corrode and fail.

Spray Cleaners

One of my favorite spray cleaners is Blue Shower. It is great for spraying the little pieces out of an amplifier chassis after you have been working on it. It is also great for cleaning control pots that have a lot of corrosion in them; I would then use DeoxIT and a silicon lube.

Spray Lubricant

This spray lubricant is great for control pots—it makes the controls work smoothly, and it doesn't gunk up after it's been there for a while. Other lubricants turn solid after a time, and make the controls bind up and make noise.

CHAPTER 2
SOLDERING

The art of making a good solder joint is essential to anyone who wants to make or modify electronic equipment. It is an art form that is not too hard to master once the basics are learned. Without good solder joints, none of your projects will have a chance to perform to their potential.

To start, you need the proper equipment. This means, at minimum, a soldering iron and solder. When working with components such as resistors, capacitors, transistors, and integrated circuits (a.k.a. ICs), I recommend using a low-wattage iron (20 to 35 watts) or a variable soldering iron. For large connectors, speaker terminals, and amplifier chassis, I suggest a higher-wattage soldering gun. Ungar and Weller have variable temperature control solder stations that can be set for any kind of soldering job.

I strongly suggest that you never use one of these stations to solder the terminals on the speakers in a cabinet. The reason is that most solder stations control their solder tips with magnetics. When you get the soldering iron close to the speaker magnets, it will demagnetize the iron, cause it to go into thermal runaway and literally melt the iron, turning your hundred-dollar solder station into junk. That's why I suggest the soldering gun or a cheap (40-watt) soldering iron.

It is advisable to have a selection of tips for your soldering iron, such as a medium-sized tip for large components and control pots, and fine tips for ICs, transistors, and small and heat-sensitive components. Any tip should be tinned the first time it is turned on and heated up. Apply a thin coat of solder to the tip and let it sit for a minute. This will protect the tip from oxidation and corrosion. Keep a damp sponge near the soldering area to wipe the hot tip between uses. A good rule is to wipe the tip and then use it to solder. *Do not solder, wipe the tip with a sponge, and put it away!* This will take the protective coating off the tip, which will cause it to corrode very quickly.

There is more than one type of solder. A 60/40 solder contains 60 percent tin and 40 percent lead, which works great for most projects. There is 63/37 solder, which has a lower melting point and hardens to a uniform surface. There are also silver solders that are used by some high-end stereo manufacturers. These solders are four percent silver mixed with tin and lead. Most solders have a hollow core that is filled with rosin flux. This flux material removes metal oxides from the surface of the components and allows the solder to adhere better. Always use flux solder—*never use acid-core solder*. Solder comes in a variety of diameters: .016, .020, .032, etc. I suggest using .032 and larger for control pots and speaker terminals where you need a lot of solder, and .020 for small components and ICs.

The trick to a great solder joint is to heat the component, and then add the solder while the soldering iron is still applying heat. Too many people apply heat, take the iron away, and then apply solder. This will surely give you an unreliable *cold-solder joint*. Think of soldering as "micro-welding." You are heating all of the surfaces to a temperature so that they can fuse together when you add the solder.

The idea is to heat the surfaces as quickly as you can, apply the minimum amount of solder needed, don't shake, and move on before you bake your part and destroy it. A cold-solder joint is cloudy, dull, and has a crusty appearance. A good solder joint is shiny, smooth, and mechanically strong.

Some old components such as vintage tube sockets, old capacitors, and resistors have corroded leads from when they were pre-tinned at the factory. You might have to take steel wool or sandpaper to the leads. I have found that an X-Acto knife works great for old tube sockets—just be careful not to cut yourself. Practice makes perfect, so practice!

Making a Guitar Cable

So many people have asked me how to make a guitar cable. It's not a hard operation—it just takes a few steps to make a great cord. Here's how you do it.

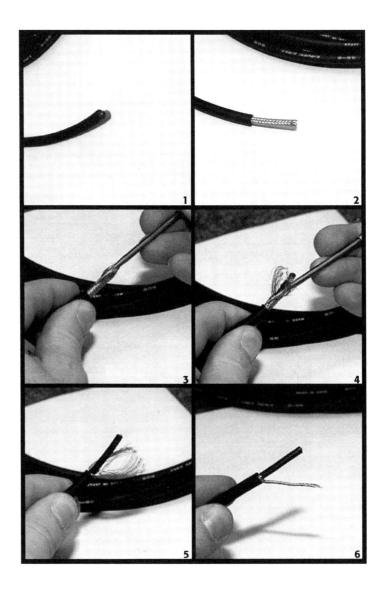

1. Here's what your cable should look like to begin with.

2. Prepare the wire by cutting off about 3/4" of the insulation. Ring the cable jacket with a sharp blade; be careful not to cut through the braided shield.

3. Pull the insulating cover off, push the braid back to loosen it, and then work a pointed tool (e.g., an awl) through the braid.

4. Part the strands without breaking any of the individual strands.

5. Separate the braid from the center wire.

6. Twist the braid together.

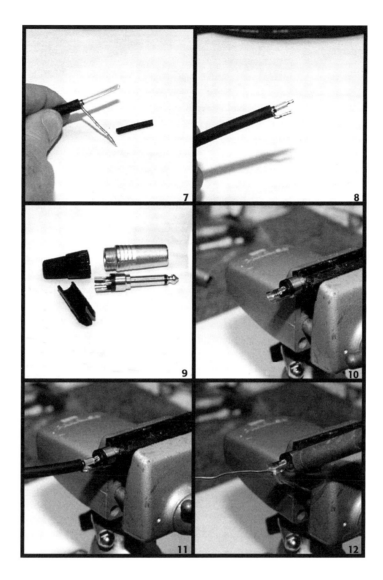

7. Some cables have a second ground shield around the center wire. Be sure to remove it. If this shield is not removed, it will cause the cable to sound muffled. Trim the insulation off the center wire. Be careful not to cut into the fine inner wires because some of the older cables have a fine fiber mixed with the inner wire. Cut this off if it's present, twist the inner wires together, and tin with solder.

8. Cut the wires to size for the connector.

9. Get your connector parts together, and make sure to put the cable cover on the cable before you solder on the connector end.

10. Put the jack end in a vise.

11. Check to make sure that the cable wire is cut correctly to fit the connector.

12. Pre-tin the jack with solder.

13. Solder the cable shield against the connector ground.

14. Solder the center (hot) terminal of the cable to the connector.

15. Check your connector for a solid, shiny solder joint. If it's not up to snuff, solder it again until the joint looks right.

16. Put the inner protective shield or strain relief on.

17. Assemble the rest of the parts, making sure to tighten them well.

18. The finished cord.

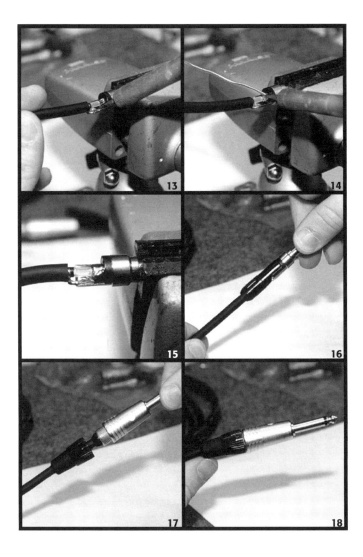

You can test the cord by using an ohmmeter to see if you have a short. Set the meter for low resistance, and then put the positive lead on one of the cable connector tips and the ground lead of the ohmmeter on the other end to see if there is connection. Also, check between the tip of the cable and the ground or shield of the cable to make sure that there isn't any connection between them. Another simple way to check the cable is to plug it into an amplifier. If there is no sound, check each end for a short.

Making a Speaker Cable

Speaker cables are made the same way that guitar cables are made. The differences are that there is not a shield or a braid, and that the wire and the connector are usually larger in size. Follow the same steps as you would to make a guitar cable, above.

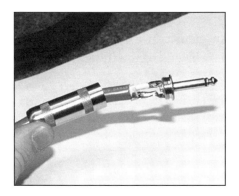

CHAPTER 3
TUBES 101

This section will cover basic vacuum tube terminology. By the time you are finished reading this section, you should know the difference between a triode (12AX7, 12AT7, 12AU7, etc.) and a beam power tube (6V6, 6L6, 6550, etc.). I'll try not to bore you with explanations that are too technical. As for the tech heads, you'll have to put up with my breaking things down for everyone to understand.

Tube Basics

All tubes have the same basic components: a filament or heater, a cathode, a grid, and a plate. Oh, yes, and for the tech heads, a getter. I'm going to give you some explanations of what goes on with these components so that later on in the book you will have a good idea why and how you are using the different pins on your tubes. So here we go—get your tech hat on.

Filament

A *filament* is an element in a directly-heated vacuum tube; a filament emits electron particles.

Heater

A *heater* is a coiled element used to heat the cathode element in an indirectly-heated vacuum tube. Indirectly-heated cathodes are always composed of oxide-coated material. The cathode is a *cylinder*—a type of sleeve that encloses a twisted wire filament. The only function of the filament is to heat the cathode. Some schematics do not show heaters and heater connections, but the heaters, of course, are still present in the tubes. The heater is not considered to be an active element. For example, a tube with an indirectly-heated cathode and a plate is still called a *diode*, even though it might seem that there are three elements in the tube.

Now, didn't that tell you a lot?

Be aware that, while some companies and tech heads call these parts "heaters," others refer to them as "filaments." Since most of the tubes out there (12AX7, 12AT7, 6V6, 6L6, 6550, etc.) do indirectly heat their cathodes, we will refer to them throughout the rest of the book as "heaters."

Heaters are generally powered by 6.3 VAC. Some of the triodes (12AX7, 12AT7, etc.) can be powered on 12.6 VAC. Heaters also have what is called a *current draw*, which is the amount of current or amperage it takes to heat the cathode. Tubes such as 12AX7, 12AT7, and 12AU7, draw about 300 ma (*milleamperes*) at 6.3 VAC and 150 ma at 12.6 VDC. Output or beam power tubes draw more current. The 6L6 draws 900 ma, the 6550 draws about 1600 ma, the 6CA7 draws 1500 ma, and the 6V6 draws about 500 ma.

I have been asked what I think about running the heaters on DC. I think it is great if you can do it. AC heaters induce hum into the circuit, and you can't get rid of it. Though there are things that you can do to make it better, it will always be there. If all you did to a stock amplifier was change the AC heaters to DC, you would hear how much quieter the DC heaters were.

Cathode

The *cathode* is the sleeve surrounding the heater in a vacuum tube. The surface of the cathode is coated with thoriated tungsten or barium oxide to increase the emission of electron particles.

Thorium

When mixed with tungsten in the form of a filament, *thorium* is a profuse emitter of electrons. Thorium is a rare mineral and will gradually evaporate during the life of the tube.

Barium Oxide

Barium oxide is a rare earth substance used in a manner similar to thorium for coating the surface of a cathode. The cathode along with the plate resistor sets the overall gain and frequency response of tubes such as 12AX7, 12AT7, 12AU7, etc. Once the heaters warm up the cathode, it emits a steady stream of electrons toward the plate. As you will see later, the cathode plays a big part in giving different amplifiers their distinct sound.

Control Grid

A *control grid* is a spiral wire placed between the plate and the cathode to which the input signal is applied. This controls the flow of electrons between the cathode and the plate.

Suppressor Grid

A *suppressor grid* is another element situated between the plate and the screen grid. Its purpose is to prevent secondary electrons emitted by the plate from striking the screen grid. The suppressor grid is generally connected to the ground or the cathode.

Screen Grid

You will find *screen grids* in pentode-type tubes; they are situated between the control grid and the plate. The screen grid is maintained at a positive potential to reduce the capacitance existing between the plate and the control grid. It acts as a shield to prevent oscillation and feedback within the tube. The screen grid can be thought of as a "force field." As you apply signal to the control grid, the field opens and closes, allowing electrons to flow from the cathode to the plate; the purpose of the grid is to control the flow of plate current. When a tube is used as an amplifier, a negative DC voltage is usually applied to the grid. Under this condition, the grid does not draw appreciable current. The number of electrons attracted to the plate depends on the combined effect of the grid and the plate polarities. When the plate is positive, as is normal, and the DC grid voltage becomes increasingly negative, the plate is less able to attract electrons, and plate current decreases. When the grid becomes less negative and increasingly positive, the plate more readily attracts electrons, and the plate current increases. When the voltage on the grid is varied in accordance with the signal, the plate current varies with the signal.

Plate

The *plate* is a flat piece of metal. Plates must be able to hold up under the heat caused by the flow of plate currents and the proximity of cathodes. Plates also need to be strong enough to withstand mechanical shocks produced by vibration and handling. Some typical materials used for electron tube plates are tungsten, molybdenum, graphite, nickel, tantalum, and copper.

Envelope

The *envelope* of a tube may be made of ceramic, metal, or glass. Its purpose is to maintain the vacuum inside the tube. The reason for this is that the heated filament would otherwise burn up in the atmosphere.

Getter

The *getter* is a silver spot that you may sometimes see on the inside surface of the glass envelope of a vacuum tube. This is normal—it is caused by the flashing of a chemical during the manufacture of the tube. Burning the chemical helps to produce a better vacuum and eliminates any remaining gases.

Triode

When a third electrode—called the *grid*—is placed between the cathode and the plate, the tube is known as a *triode.* The grid usually consists of relatively fine wire wound on two support rods, extending the length of the cathode. The spacing between turns of wire is large compared with the size of the wire, so that the passage of electrons from cathode to plate is practically unobstructed by the grid.

Tetrode

With the addition of the second grid, a tube will have four electrodes and will accordingly be called a *tetrode.* The second screen grid is mounted between the first grid (the control grid) and the plate, and acts as an electrostatic shield between them, thus reducing the grid-to-plate capacitance. The effectiveness of this shield is increased by a bypass capacitor between the screen grid and the cathode. The screen grid has another desirable effect: It makes the plate current practically independent of the plate voltage (over a certain range). The screen grid is operated at a positive voltage and, therefore, attracts electrons from the cathode. As long as the plate voltage is higher than the screen grid voltage, the plate current in a screen grid tube depends to a large degree on the screen grid voltage and very little on the plate voltage. This fact makes it possible to obtain much higher amplification with a tetrode than with a triode.

Pentodes

A *pentode* is a five-electrode tube. In power output pentodes, the suppressor grid makes possible higher power output with lower grid-driving voltage. In radio frequency amplifier pentodes, the suppressor grid makes high voltage amplification possible at moderate values of plate voltage. These desirable features result from the fact that the plate voltage swing can be made very large. The plate voltage may be as low as, or lower than, the screen grid voltage without loss in signal gain capability.

Beam Power Tubes

A *beam power tube* is a tetrode or pentode in which directed electron beams are used to substantially increase the power handling capability of a tube. Such a tube contains a cathode, a control grid, a screen grid, a plate, and a suppressor grid. When a beam power tube is designed without an actual suppressor grid, the electrodes are so spaced that the secondary emission from the plate is suppressed by space-charged effects between the screen, grid, and plate. The space charge is produced by the slowing down of electrons traveling from a high potential screen grid to a lower potential plate. In this low velocity region, the space charge produced is sufficient to repel secondary electrons emitted from the plate and to cause them to return to the plate. Beam power tubes of this design employ beam-confining electrodes at cathode potential to assist in producing the desired beam effects and to prevent stray electrons from the plate from returning to the screen grid outside of the beam.

Tube Symbols

SYMBOLS THIS TEXT	MEANING	OTHER TEXTS
E_p	PLATE VOLTAGE , D.C. VALUE	
E_{bb}	PLATE SUPPLY VOLTAGE , D.C.	B+
E_c	GRID BIAS VOLTAGE, D.C. VALUE	E_g
E_{cc}	GRID BIAS SUPPLY VOLTAGE , D.C.	C−
e_p	INSTANTANEOUS PLATE VOLTAGE	
e_c	INSTANTANEOUS GRID VOLTAGE	
e_g	A.C. COMPONENT OF GRID VOLTAGE	
e_p	A.C. COMPONENT OF PLATE VOLTAGE (ANODE)	
I_p	D.C. PLATE CURRENT	
R_p	D.C. PLATE RESISTANCE	
R_g	GRID RESISTANCE	
R_k	CATHODE RESISTANCE	
R_L	LOAD RESISTANCE	

The above chart lists electron tube symbols. You will have cause to use these letters and abbreviations to symbolize electrical quantities.

The History of the Vacuum Tube

<u>Lee de Forest and the Audion</u>

One night in September 1900, Lee de Forest was working with a sponder in his gaslit room and noticed something very strange. When he operated the key of the spark transmitter, the gaslight flickered. He immediately called his assistant to observe this phenomenon and together they pondered its significance. Their first conclusion was that the flickering flame represented a new type of detector action that might overcome many of the problems that plagued the sponder. The two excited experimenters watched the flame respond to the keying of the transmitter and took detailed notes for several weeks. When the transmitter was moved to another room and the door was closed, the flickering of the flame stopped. It then became clear that the flame was responding to the sound waves generated by the spark transmitter and not to electromagnetic waves.

Lee de Forest stopped the flame experiments. He later claimed that the flickering flame started a train of thought that ultimately led to his developing the "Triode Audion." Lee de Forest believed that the gases ionized by the flame produced the relay action. The flame itself was only the mechanism for producing the gas ionization needed. Other means of heating the gases sufficient to produce ionization would result in the same detector action. The best way to obtain a stable detector, de Forest reasoned, was to place the electrodes in a glass envelope and heat the gases to ionization with an external Bunsen burner, or to pass an electrical current through carbon or tantalum filaments. Both heating techniques were tried. Lee de Forest quickly realized the advantages of filament heating. The air inside the envelope was evacuated only to the point where the filament would not be oxidized when heated. A sodium or potassium salt was placed inside the envelope to produce increased ionization.

Lee de Forest was convinced that his Audion's sensitivity as a detector could be increased even more. Remembering the improvement the separate local circuit had made in his flame detector, he added an additional plate outside of the glass envelope. The external plate provided what de Forest called "electrostatic control" for the detector. He then built a similar device with a coil on the outside of the glass envelope, which produced "electromagnetic control." The next Audion he built had two separate internal plates. The plates were located on opposite sides of the filament and the second plate was used as the control element. Lee de Forest was amazed with the performance of the Audion. A patent application on this first Triode Audion was filed on October 25, 1906. Lee de Forest was granted the patent on January 15, 1907.

It didn't take long for de Forest to realize that the control element should exert an even greater effect if it were located between the filament and plate. A solid control element would block the flow of current. A zigzag wire arrangement was used and eventually developed into the grid found in today's tubes. The three-element "Grid Audion" proved to be a much better detector. This three-element circuit was included with his January 29, 1907 Grid Audion patent application; the patent was granted on February 18, 1908.

And that's how Lee de Forest's most famous and most important Audion was born. The potential usefulness of the three-element Triode Audion was not immediately apparent. The Triode Audion was expensive and its filament life was relatively short. In Lee de Forest's 1906 patent application, he called the original Triode Audion a "device for amplifying feeble electric currents." The techniques necessary for making it function as a true amplifier would not be developed for another six years.

Lee de Forest and his co-workers achieved amplification in 1912 by using audio frequency transformers to couple the signal to and from the Audion. They found it extremely beneficial to reduce further the already low pressure inside the envelope. In time, the Audion's spherical shape would become tubular, and the generic name for this and similar devices would become the *vacuum tube*. In the course of developing the amplifier, de Forest found that his circuit oscillated—a phenomenon commonly encountered by amplifier builders today. The discovery that the Triode could be used as an amplifier or as an oscillator established it as a truly important electronic device.

The Tube Revival

In early 1983, the tube revival in the audio industry began to swing into full gear. In the years since, we've seen the prices of vintage tube gear skyrocket. You can find tubes in everything now, from small practice amplifiers to the most sophisticated high-end, pro-audio studio effects. In 1991, the last large scale manufacturer of quality audio tubes in United States, MPD of Owensboro, Kentucky, stopped manufacturing tubes—including General Electric's 6550A, 6CA7, 6L6GC, 6V6, etc. I was designing for Ampeg when we got the call. We were informed that there was going to be an end to our tube supply, especially the 6550A. Well, we made the same decision that a lot of other amp manufacturers did, and we bought all that we could get our hands on! This worked for a while, but as you have probably noticed, most of the amplifier companies have run out of stock of their precious booty by now.

There are companies out there that still have stock left, and there are a couple of new companies that have sprung up that are producing good tubes. Richardson Electronics of LaFox, Illinois is one of the largest tube distributors in the country. Richardson bought a huge lifetime supply of GE products before MPD ceased their production—they have the product and they are asking top dollar for it. They have 6550A, 6L6GC, 6CA7, 7591, 12BH7, 12AX7, and 12AT7 tubes, to name a few of the popular ones. Antique Electronic Supply, oriented toward the radio collector market, stocks several thousand tube types and prices are reasonable. Ram Tubes offers a full range of selected and matched tubes, including *NOS.* (new old stock). Their prices are high, but they offer a good warranty. VTL offers a fair price on some of the most popular brands. They even claim their KT-90 is better than the 6550A (I haven't tried it, but it's hard to beat the original GE 6550A!). Triode Electronics sell a good variety of NOS and foreign exotics. Elmira Electronics has a wide range of Westinghouse brand tubes geared for the repair market. New Sensor supplies music dealers and manufacturers. They have great pricing, but you must be a dealer or manufacturer. PM Components has a good stock of NOS British tubes, as well as newer stuff. They offer matching and in house testing. Groove Tubes has a great supply of tubes—everything from NOS to brand new stock. Groove Tubes is like Richardson and New Sensor: You must be a dealer or manufacturer to purchase from them. The U.S. government was the largest purchaser of electron tubes in the world, so their many military auctions are now the best places to find NOS GE and Sylvania tubes.

Notes on Specific Tubes

EL-34/6CA7

Introduced in 1950 by Mullard Ltd. in England, this model has a soft vacuum and a plate voltage rated to 800 V. It has a little metal collar around the brown base and a high transconductance, and it allows up to 100 watts output. The Type Two Mullard had a straight-sided black or brown Bakelite base without a metal collar. The Type Three looks almost the same, except that its assembly is funky—the main structure of the tube is crimped instead of welded.

East Germany makes an EL-34. Their tube is characterized by a deep, round dimple on the top of the bulb and a crimped plate structure. These tubes have been branded as ITT Schaub-Lorenz, Marshall, National Semiconductors, RCA, Siemens, and Telefunken. There was an EL-34 manufactured in China, but all I can say about that one is "run away and don't look back." I bought several thousand of these when they first came out and most (and I do mean *most*) of them went into runaway with the plates glowing cherry red and failed shortly afterwards like a 4th of July spectacle.

The Sylvania 6CA7 is the best bet for 6CA7s: It's US-made, very reliable, and rugged. It has a big bulb close to the GE 6L6. The 6CA7 is the closest cross between the British EL-34 and the US GE6550. It's not as harsh as the 6550, and has a better, tight bottom end than the EL-34. The only problem is that it's hard to find Sylvania 6CA7s. There are some people out there who still have stock. And if you find any, you'd better buy them up before Eddy V. finds them—it's his tube of choice.

6550A

Introduced in the 1950s, the best version of the 6550 ever made was a Coke bottle–shaped tube from Tung Sol. The Tung Sol 6550 has a nickel-plated, solid copper collar around a brown Bakelite base; it has been branded as Dynaco, Magnavox, RCA, Tung Sol, and Warner Electric. This tube is the most popular of the 6550s but is only found as NOS and (if it's found at all) is expensive. Don't worry about how old these tubes may be, as long as they are in new condition or have not been used much. I have seen 35-year-old Tung Sols sound better than the most recent stock of GE6550s.

The next best 6550 is the GE6550, made by MPD for General Electric. This tube has been the workhorse of the industry. Ampeg used it in their SVT bass amp series because of its great tight low-end response and high power output. This tube is characterized by its straight-sided glass envelope, dome-topped bulb, black plastic base with a nickel-plated metal collar, and a crimped plate construction.

Phillips made a 6550 similar to the GE6550, but with a slimmer bulb. This tube is also found only as NOS. Lastly, there is also the Chinese 6550A, which looks identical to the old Tung Sol tube. They obviously tried to copy it, but the survey says that it isn't even close. This tube lacks bottom and top, and sounds almost like a GE when it's going bad. The only difference is that the Chinese tube is more prone to failure (so it's a great tube for target practice!).

KT-88

As you may have noticed, the '50s were popular with tube manufacturers for producing high-powered pentodes. The M.O. Valve Company of England produced one of the best KT-88s to date, which is highly sought after by collectors in America and Japan. This tube is characterized by a very large glass bulb with straight sides, stepping into a dome-shaped top and a silver metal collar around a brown Bakelite base. This tube is definitely the workhorse of the industry. Rated at 42 watts at 800 V, a single pair of KT-88s can provide 150 watts of audio power. The KT-88 offers less than two percent total harmonic distortion (THD) up to near full output, and can be used as a substitute for the GE6550A. Richardson Electronics produced a limited re-issue of the original KT-88; I used a pair of these in Paul Gilbert's modified Marshall 50-watt heads and they sounded great. Groove Tubes has their version of the tube, too.

6L6GC/5881

The 6L6, designed by RCA as a linear output tube, had a metal envelope. As glassblowing equipment improved, this allowed consistent quality and a better vacuum. This tube was then known as the 6L6B, and the industrial version of this tube was called the 5881, which had a rugged internal construction with mica stiffeners. The 5881 was used in old Fender amplifiers; they were known to clip a little sooner than the 6L6, when pushed. They also had more of a mid-range tone, which was coined as being the sound of early rock. The 5881 was introduced by Tung Sol in the 1950s, with a more compact, higher-gain version than the 6L6. Again, this tube can only be found as NOS, if you're lucky. Sovtek of Russia makes a good 5881, featuring a heavy glass bulb and a good internal construction. I've used them in production on my Lee Jackson Amplifiers and have had very few failures; they can also handle very high plate voltages with minimal probability of them flaming out. After World War II, the M.O. Valve Company produced their version of the 6L6 and called it the KT-66. They're marked with the following brands: Emitron, Genalex, Gold Lion, I.E.C., M.W.T, and Mullard. These, if you can find them, are NOS. General Electric offers a modern version of the KT-66, designated 7581, which resembles and sounds very close to the original.

The 6L6GC represented a leap in performance levels from 360 V to 550 V anode rating, and from 23 watts to 30 watts plate dissipation. The GC (which stands for "glass container") became the workhorse for most of the music industry. Sylvania has one of the best 6L6s, which was especially designed for Fender to hang upside down inside a cabinet. The 6L6GC became the standard for companies such as Acoustic, Boogie, Mitchell, and Peavey; even some early Marshalls had 6L6s. The 6L6 family of tubes has a subdued high end and great low end, and is liked by blues, grunge, and metal players alike. The slightly subdued high end of the 6L6 is also popular with country players.

6V6

This tube is the most common power tube used in amplifiers that are manufactured in the United States. The 6V6 has a sweet, creamy tone, which makes it great for low volume gigs or studio recording. The 6V6 is one of my favorite tubes. I used it in the Crate Stealth Series and found that it not only sounded great at low volumes, but it also rocked when cranked up. The 6V6 is similar to the 6L6, but delivers 15 watts to the 6L6s 22 watts. Because most amplifiers that use 6V6s have a compatible bias with the 6L6, you can interchange them to your liking. I have even interchanged amplifiers that use four 6L6s to use two 6L6s and two 6V6s; make sure that the plate voltages don't exceed the 6V6 specs.

6BQ5/EL-84

The EL-84 is a nine-pin, miniature version of the EL-34. Although it has a similar electrical range to the 6V6, it doesn't sound close. The EL-84 has a glassy, crisp sound with a great shimmery top end. The EL-84 is found in lots of vintage, low-powered amplifiers from the 1960s. The Vox AC 30 amps—which were used by the Beatles and Brian May of Queen—have a very distinct tone because of the EL-84.

7027A

The 7027A is a highly linear power tube; General Electric manufactured them for the North American market. These tubes were hard vacuumed, which made them too clean sounding for the discriminating guitar player. The 7027A was popular with the bass amplifier made by Traynor, although it was dropped by most due to the extreme unit cost. The good news is that most amplifiers that used the 7027A can be converted to use GE6550s.

12AX7a/7025/ECC83

There have been hundreds of variations in this type of tube since its introduction in the 1940s. Known as *preamp tubes*, these tubes have been the most popular *high-mu* (high amplification), miniature, twin triodes used by amplifier manufacturers around the world. Because these two tubes are so equipment (i.e., circuit) dependent, it is really hard to explain what the differences are among them.

The 7025 is the military version of the 12AX7 with lower noise and better microphonics—now, this can mean anything the tube supplier wants to tell you, since it's literally impossible to find the original 7025s. I have found that some tube suppliers have rescreened 12AX7s and ECC83s with "7025" on them. The Chinese 12AX7 has become the tube of choice to rescreen with 7025. I have found these tubes to have high gain, low noise, and fair microphonics. You will have to test and select for first-position preamp circuits, since I have also found that the glass bulb varies in diameter from run to run—this is why I changed over to the Russian 12AX7. The early GE 12AX7s and the new Russian 12AX7s seem to be the closest match, with a soft warm sound that has more mid range and good gain. I have found the Russian 12AX7 to be good with the microphonics and pretty quiet per case box.

The ECC83—made by Amperex and called "Bugle Boy"—was introduced in the 1950s, and was very popular with British manufacturers (and American ones as well when U.S. supplies were low). The Mullard ECC83, also manufactured in the 1950s, was said to be specifically designed for audio. These remain the most favored with guitarists who use British-made amplifiers such as Hiwatt, Marshall, and Vox. One thing is for sure: All are interchangeable and can be mixed and matched in various permutations until you find the sound you personally like.

12AT7

This tube may be found in most of the older Fender amps. It is used in the reverb driver position and as the phase inverter drive tube. It is also a high-mu, twin triode with a slightly higher drive current—this makes it sound cleaner both in the reverb and phase inverter driver position. I, personally, like it as a reverb driver, but similar to the 12AX7, it's better as a phase inverter driver. The 12AT7 and the 12AX7 are interchangeable in every position. It's up to your discerning ear. The military equivalence is the 6201.

12AU7A

The 12AU7 is similar to the 12AT7, but has a little more gain or output and is used in phase inverters on high-power amplifiers. You can find 12AU7s in Ampeg, Leslie, and Macintoshes. You can substitute 12AX7s and 12AT7s for 12AU7s, if needed.

12AY7

This tube, used in Fender and Gibson amplifiers, was popular in the late 1940s and early 1950s. It has the same gain as the early 12AX7s. Fender replaced it with the 12AX7 because of its better availability. The military equivalent of the 12AY7 is the 6072.

12DW7

This tube is a dual triode, containing high- and medium-mu triodes. It was popular with Ampeg amps built by Magnavox. The 12DW7 is one of the most difficult tubes to find because of its lack of popularity in the amp companies. The 12AX7 can be substituted for the 12DW7 on the Ampeg V2, V4, V4B, VT22, and VT40. The military equivalent is the 7247.

Tube Substitutions

12AX7a

12AD7
12AU7A
12AX7A
12AX7WA
12BZ7
12DF7
12DM7
12DT7
5751
5751WA
6057
6681
6L13
7025A
7494
7729
B339
B759
CV4004
E83CC
ECC803
ECC83
M8137

12AU7

12AU7A,AW
12AX7
5814A,AW
5963
6067
6189
6670
6680
7316
7489
7730
ECC186
ECC802
ECC82
M813

12AT7

A2900
M8162
7728
B152
QA2406
12AZ7
B309
QB309
B739
6060
CV4024
6201
ECC801
6671
ECC81
6679
E81CC
7492

12AY7

6072
2082

6BQ5/EL-8

6267
6BQ5WA
6P15
7189A
EF86
E84L
N709
Z729
7320

6L6GC

5881
5932
7581A
WT6
EL-37

EL-34/6CA7

7D11
12E13
KT-77
KT-88

6550a

7D11
7027A
12E13
KT-88

CHAPTER 4

ELECTRONIC SYMBOLS
AND HELPFUL INFORMATION

RESISTOR COLOR CODE

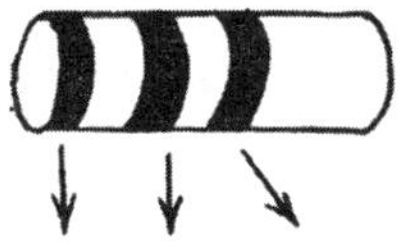

BLACK	0 0	× 1
BROWN	1 1	× 10
RED	2 2	× 100
ORANGE	3 3	× 1,000
YELLOW	4 4	× 10,000
GREEN	5 5	× 100,000
BLUE	6 6	× 1,000,000
VIOLET	7 7	× 10,000,000
GRAY	8 8	× 100,000,000
WHITE	9 9	—

FOURTH BAND INDICATES TOLERANCE
GOLD = ±5 %   SILVER = ±10%   NONE = ±20%

M (MEG-)   = × 1,000,000
K (KILO-) = × 1,000
m (MILLI-) = .001
μ (MICRO-) = .000 001
n (NANO-) = .000 000 001
p (PICO-) = .000 000 000 001

A = AMPERE   R = RESISTANCE
F = FARAD   V = VOLT
I = CURRENT   W = WATT
P = POWER   Ω = OHM

OHM'S LAW

$V = IR$ $R = VI$
$I = V/R$ $P = VI = I^2 R$

SIZE	POWER	LENGTH
	1/8 WATT	1/4 INCH
	1/2 WATT	3/8 INCH
	1 WATT	9/16 INCH
	2 WATT	11/16 INCH

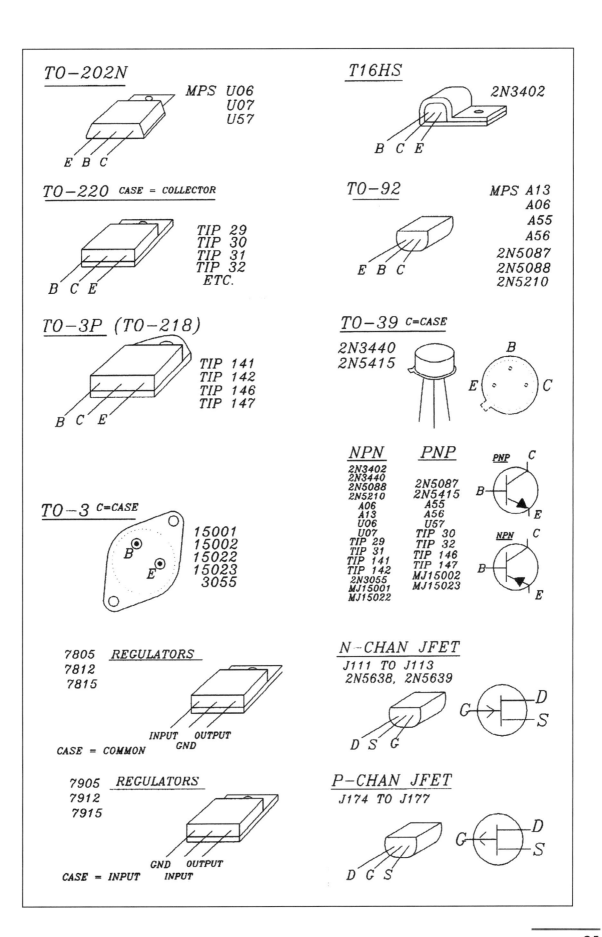

TO-202N

MPS U06
U07
U57

E B C

T16HS

2N3402

B C E

TO-220 CASE = COLLECTOR

TIP 29
TIP 30
TIP 31
TIP 32
ETC.

B C E

TO-92

MPS A13
A06
A55
A56
2N5087
2N5088
2N5210

E B C

TO-3P (TO-218)

TIP 141
TIP 142
TIP 146
TIP 147

B C E

TO-39 C=CASE

2N3440
2N5415

B
E C

TO-3 C=CASE

15001
15002
15022
15023
3055

B
E

NPN	PNP
2N3402	
2N3440	
2N5088	2N5087
2N5210	2N5415
A06	A55
A13	A56
U06	U57
U07	TIP 30
TIP 29	TIP 32
TIP 31	TIP 146
TIP 141	TIP 147
TIP 142	MJ15002
2N3055	MJ15023
MJ15001	
MJ15022	

PNP
C
B
E

NPN
C
B
E

7805 *REGULATORS*
7812
7815

INPUT OUTPUT
GND

CASE = COMMON

N-CHAN JFET
J111 TO J113
2N5638, 2N5639

D S G

G D
S

7905 *REGULATORS*
7912
7915

GND OUTPUT
INPUT

CASE = INPUT

P-CHAN JFET
J174 TO J177

D G S

G D
S

semiconductor symbols

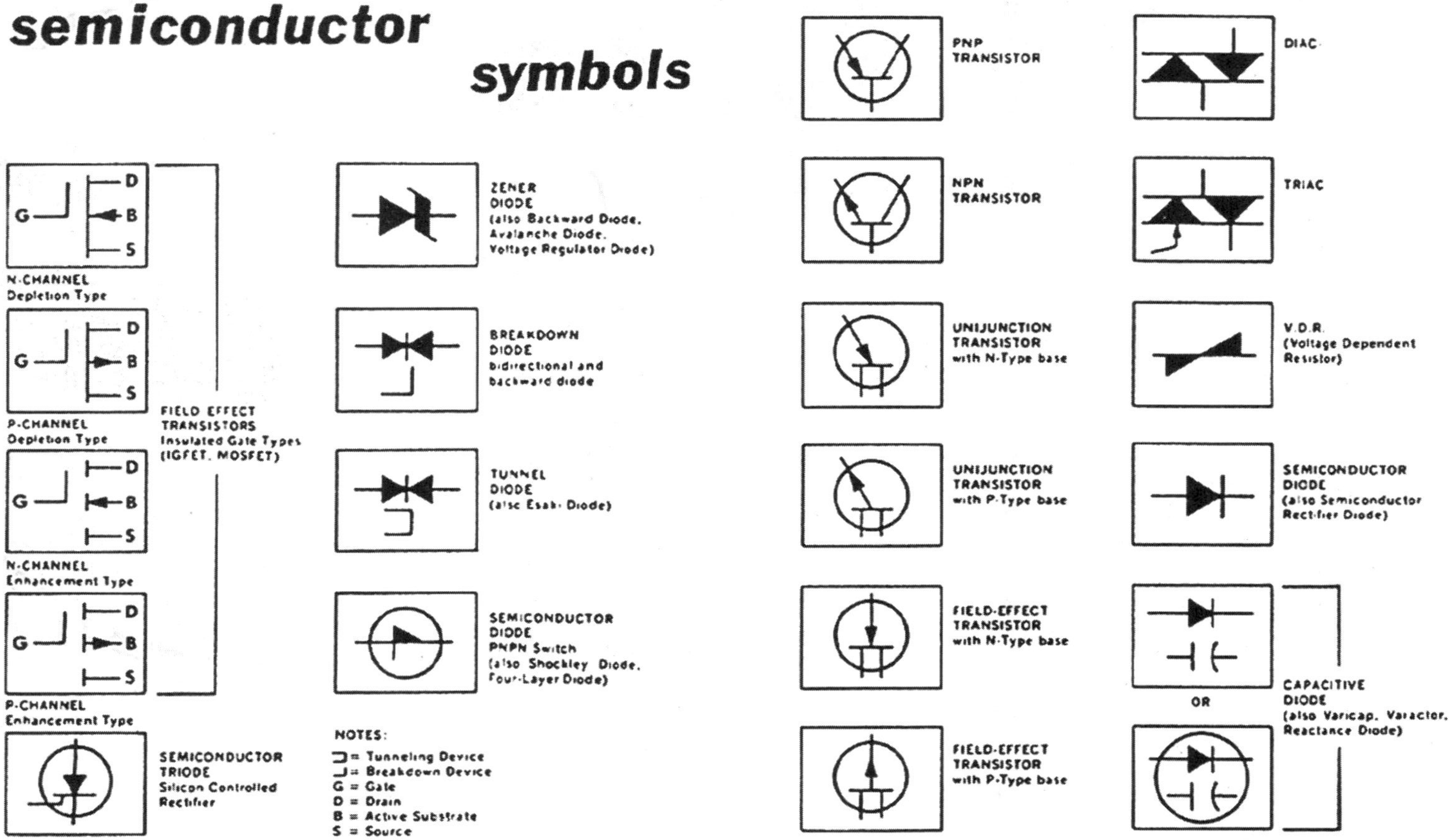

N-CHANNEL Depletion Type

P-CHANNEL Depletion Type

FIELD EFFECT TRANSISTORS Insulated Gate Types (IGFET, MOSFET)

N-CHANNEL Enhancement Type

P-CHANNEL Enhancement Type

SEMICONDUCTOR TRIODE Silicon Controlled Rectifier

ZENER DIODE (also Backward Diode, Avalanche Diode, Voltage Regulator Diode)

BREAKDOWN DIODE Bidirectional and Backward Diode

TUNNEL DIODE (also Esaki Diode)

SEMICONDUCTOR DIODE PNPN Switch (also Shockley Diode, Four-Layer Diode)

PNP TRANSISTOR

NPN TRANSISTOR

UNIJUNCTION TRANSISTOR with N-Type base

UNIJUNCTION TRANSISTOR with P-Type base

FIELD-EFFECT TRANSISTOR with N-Type base

FIELD-EFFECT TRANSISTOR with P-Type base

DIAC

TRIAC

V.D.R. (Voltage Dependent Resistor)

SEMICONDUCTOR DIODE (also Semiconductor Rectifier Diode)

CAPACITIVE DIODE (also Varicap, Varactor, Reactance Diode)

OR

FIELD-EFFECT TRANSISTOR

NOTES:

⊐ = Tunneling Device

⊐ = Breakdown Device

G = Gate

D = Drain

B = Active Substrate

S = Source

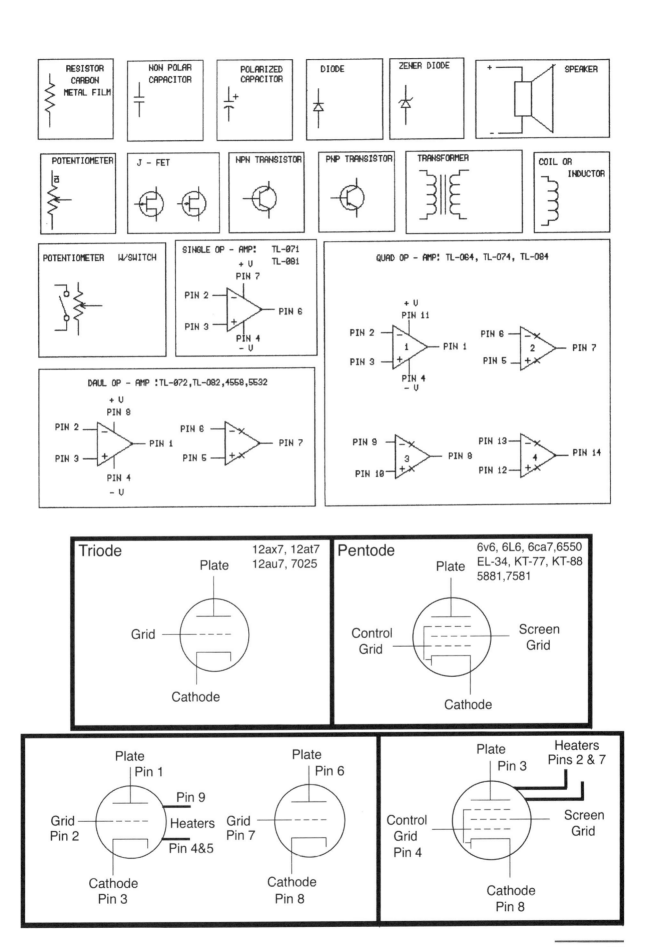

| RESISTOR CARBON METAL FILM | NON POLAR CAPACITOR | POLARIZED CAPACITOR | DIODE | ZENER DIODE | SPEAKER |

| POTENTIOMETER | J - FET | NPN TRANSISTOR | PNP TRANSISTOR | TRANSFORMER | COIL OR INDUCTOR |

POTENTIOMETER   W/SWITCH

SINGLE OP - AMP: TL-071 TL-081
+ U
PIN 7
PIN 2 −
PIN 3 +
PIN 6
PIN 4
− U

QUAD OP - AMP: TL-064, TL-074, TL-084
+ U
PIN 11
PIN 2 −
PIN 3 +
1
PIN 1
PIN 4
− U

PIN 6 −
PIN 5 +
2
PIN 7

PIN 9 −
PIN 10 +
3
PIN 8

PIN 13 −
PIN 12 +
4
PIN 14

DAUL OP - AMP :TL-072,TL-082,4558,5532
+ U
PIN 8
PIN 2 −
PIN 3 +
PIN 1
PIN 4
− U

PIN 6 −
PIN 5 +
PIN 7

Triode
12ax7, 12at7
12au7, 7025
Plate
Grid
Cathode

Pentode
6v6, 6L6, 6ca7,6550
EL-34, KT-77, KT-88
5881,7581
Plate
Control Grid
Screen Grid
Cathode

Plate
Pin 1
Pin 9
Grid
Pin 2
Heaters
Pin 4&5
Cathode
Pin 3

Plate
Pin 6
Grid
Pin 7
Cathode
Pin 8

Plate
Pin 3
Heaters
Pins 2 & 7
Control Grid
Pin 4
Screen Grid
Cathode
Pin 8

1 Pots (Potentiometers)
2 Inputs
3 Bias Adjustment
4 Bridge Rectifier
5 Diodes

6 Filter Capacitors
7 Power Tube Sockets
8 Preamp Tube Sockets
9 Fuse Holders
10 Impedance Selector

11 Speaker Outputs
12 Capacitors
13 Resistors
14 Polarity Switch
15 Power Switch

16 Standby Switch
17 Power Light

1 Power Transformer   4 Filter Capacitors   7 Speaker Outputs
2 Output Transformer   5 Power Tubes   8 Impedance Selector
3 Choke Transformer   6 Preamp Tubes   9 Fuse Holders

1 Power Transformer   7 Dual Op Amp (IC)   13 Headphone Output
2 Output Transistors   8 Capacitors   14 Line Out Jack
3 Filter Capacitors   9 Resistors   15 Power Switch
4 Bridge Rectifier   10 Emitter Resistors   16 AC Input Receptacle
5 Fuse   11 Pots (Potentiometers)   17 Speaker Outputs
6 Driver Transistors   12 Inputs

Transistor Information

Standard Transistor Markings

Joint Electron Device Engineering Council (JEDEC):
Digit, Letter, Serial Number, [Suffix]

The letter is always "N", and the first digit is one less than the number of legs ("2" for transistors). Four-legged transistors get a "3." 4N and 5N are reserved for optocouplers. The optional [Suffix] indicates the gain group of the transistor.

A	=	Low Gain
B	=	Medium Gain
C	=	High Gain
No Suffix	=	Any Gain

Japanese Industrial Standard (JIS):
Digit, Two Letters, Serial Number, [Suffix]

The first digit is one less than the number of legs. The letters indicate the application area and the type of the device.

SA	=	PNP HF Transistor
SB	=	PNP AF Transistor
SC	=	NPN HF Transistor
SD	=	NPN AF Transistor
SE	=	Diodes
SF	=	Thyristors
SG	=	Gunn Devices
SH	=	UJT
SJ	=	P-Channel FET/MOSFET
SK	=	N-Channel FET/MOSFET
SM	=	Triac
SQ	=	LED (a.k.a. light emitting diode)
SR	=	Rectifier
SS	=	Signal Diodes
ST	=	Avalanche Diodes
SV	=	Varicaps
SZ	=	Zener Diodes

Pro-Electron:
Two Letters, Letter, Serial Number, [Suffix]

The first letter indicates the material.

A = Ge
B = Si
C = GaAs
R = Compound Materials

The second letter indicates the device application.

A = Diode
B = Variac
C = Transistor, AF, Small Signal
D = Transistor, AF, Power
E = Tunnel Diode
F = Transistor, HF Small Signal
K = Hall Effect Device

Two Letters, Letter, Serial Number, [Suffix]

The first letter indicates the material. The third letter indicates that the device is intended for industrial rather than commercial applications. It is usually W, X, Y, or Z.

L = Transistor, HF, Power
N = Optocoupler
P = Radiation-Sensitive Device
Q = Radiation-Producing Device
R = Thyristor, Low Power
T = Thyristor, Power
U = Transistor, Power, Switching
Y = Rectifier
Z = Zener, Voltage Rectifier Diode

Specialist Application

MJ   = Motorola Power, Metal Case
MJE = Motorola Power, Plastic Case
MPX = Motorola Low Power, Plastic Case
MRF = Motorola HF, VHF and Microwave Transistor
RCA = RCA
RCS = RCS
TIP = Texas Instruments Power Transistor
TIPL = Texas Instruments Planar Power Transistor
TIS = Texas Instruments Small Signal Transistor

Symbol	Notation
A	Amperes (a-c, rms, or d-c)
A	Amplifier voltage gain
a	Amperes (peak)
ac, a-c, a.c.	Alternating current
a-m, a.m.	Amplitude modulation
C	Capacitance
c.f.m.	Cubic feet per minute
C_{gg}	Capacitance grid to ground
C_{gk}, C_{gp}, etc.	Tube capacitance between indicated electrodes
C_{in}	Input capacitance
C_k	Capacitance between cathode and ground
cm	Centimeter
C_N	Neutralizing capacitance
C_{out}	Output capacitance
C_{pg2}	Capacitance, plate to screen
cw, c.w. or c-w	Continuous wave
dB or db	Decibel
dc, d.c., d-c	Direct current
E	Voltage (a-c, rms, or d-c)
e	Peak voltage
E_b	Average plate voltage
e_b	Instantaneous plate voltage
$e_{b\ max}$	Peak plate voltage
$e_{b\ min}$	Minimum instantaneous plate voltage referenced to ground
$e_{c\ mp}$	Maximum positive grid voltage
E_{co}	Cutoff-bias voltage
E_{c1}	Average grid #1 voltage
E_{c2}	Average grid #2 voltage
E_{c3}	Average grid #3 voltage
e_{c1}	Instantaneous grid #1 voltage
e_{c2}	Instantaneous grid # 2 voltage
e_{c3}	Instantaneous grid #3 voltage
E_f	Filament voltage
e_g	Rms value of exciting voltage
e_p	Instantaneous plate voltage (a.c.) referenced to E_b
$e_{p\ max}$	Peak a-c plate voltage referenced to E_b
E_{sig}	Applied signal voltage (d-c)
e_{sig}	Applied signal voltage (a-c)
e_k	Instantaneous cathode voltage
$e_{k\ max}$	Peak cathode voltage
F	Farad
f	Frequency (in Hertz)

Symbol	Notation
fil	Filament
G	Giga (10^9)
g, g_1, g_2, etc.	Grid (number to identify, starting from cathode)
$g_{2,1}$	Grids having common pin connection
GHz	Gigahertz (10^9 cycles per second)
G_m or S_m	Transconductance (grid-plate)
H	Henry
Hz	Hertz
i	Peak current
I	Current (a-c, rms, or d-c)
I_b	Average d-c plate current
$I_{b\ max}$	Peak signal d-c plate current
i_b	Instantaneous plate current
$i_{b\ max}$	Peak plate current
I_{bo}	Idling plate current
I_c	Average d-c grid current current
i_p	Instantaneous a-c plate current referred to I_b
$i_{p\ max}$	Peak a-c plate current referred to I_b
i_1 etc.	Fundamental component of r-f plate current
$i_{1\ max}$	Peak fundamental component of r-f plate current
I_1	Single tone d-c plate current
I_2 etc.	Two-tone, etc., d-c plate current
$I_{c1,\ c2}$, etc.	Average grid #1, #2, etc. current
I_f	Filament current
i_{g1}, i_{g2} etc.	Instantantous grid current
$i_{g1\ max}$, etc.	Peak grid current
I_k	Average cathode current
i_k	Instantaneous cathode current
$i_{k\ max}$	Peak cathode current
K	Cathode
k	Kilo(10^3)
kHz	Kilohertz
kV	Peak kilovolts
kVac	A-c kilovolts
kVdc	D-c kilovolts
kW	Kilowatts
λ	Wavelength
M	Mutual inductance
M	Mega (10^6)
m	Meter
m	One thousandth

Symbol	Notation
mm	Millimeter
mA or ma	Milliamperes
Meg or meg	Megohm
mH	Millihenry
MHz	Megahertz
Mu or μ	Amplification factor
mV or mv	Millivolts
MW	Megawatts
mW	Milliwatts
NF	Noise figure
N_p	Efficiency
p	Pico (10^{-12})
P_d	Average drive power
p_d	Peak drive power
P_{ft}	Average feedthrough power
p_{ft}	Peak feedthrough power
pF or pf	Picofarad
PEP	Peak envelope power
P_{g1}, P_{g2}, etc.	Power dissipation of respective grids
P_i	Power input (average)
p_i	Peak power input
P_o	Power output (average)
p_o	Peak power output
P_p	Plate dissipation
Q	Figure of merit
Q_L	Loaded Q
R	Resistance
r	Reflector
rf, r.f. or r-f	Radio frequency
R_g	Resistance in series with the grid.
r_g	Dynamic internal grid resistance
R_k	Resistance in series with the cathode
R_L	Load resistance
rms	Root mean square

Symbol	Notation
R_p	Resistance in series with plate
r_p	Dynamic internal plate resistance
S_c or G_c	Conversion transconductance
S_m or G_m	Transconductance
SSB	Single sideband
SWR	Standing-wave ratio
T	Temperature (°C)
t	Time (seconds)
θ	Conduction angle
μ	Micro (10^{-6}) or amplification factor
μ	Amplification Factor
μA	Microampere
μmho	Micromho
μF or μfd	Microfarad
μH	Microhenry
μs	Microsecond
μV	Microvolt
μ_{sg}	Grid-screen amplification factor
V	Volt(s), (a-c, rms, or d-c) or d.c.)
v	Peak volts
Vac	A-c volts
Vdc	D-c volts
VSWR	Voltage standing-wave ratio
W	Watts
Z	Impedance
Z_g	Grid impedance
Z_i	Input impedance
Z_k	Cathode impedance
Z_L	Load impedance
Z_o	Output impedance
Z_p	Impedance in plate circuit
Z_x	Screen bypass impedance

Change of dB	Power	Voltage
0	1	1
1	1.3	1.1
2	1.6	1.3
3	2	1.4
4	2.5	1.6
5	3.2	1.8
6	4	2
7	5	2.2
8	6.3	2.5
9	8	2.8
10	10	3.2
11	12.6	3.5
12	16	4
15	32	5.6
18	64	8
20	100	10
30	1000	31.6
40	10000	100
50	100000	316.2
60	1000000	1000
70	10000000	3162.3
80	100000000	10000
90	1000000000	31622.8
100	10000000000	100000
110	100000000000	316227.8
120	1000000000000	1000000

Voltage Rated in Decibels

Decibels can be used to measure sound pressure levels. They can also be used to determine power ratios. Unfortunately, the "3dB = twice as much power" rule does not apply to voltage. Instead, a new ratio scale for voltage is used. The dB scale must use a reference figure. There are two commonly used voltage references: dBV, where 0 dB is equal to 1 V, and dBU, where 0 dB is equal to .775 V. dBV is used for any voltage comparison.

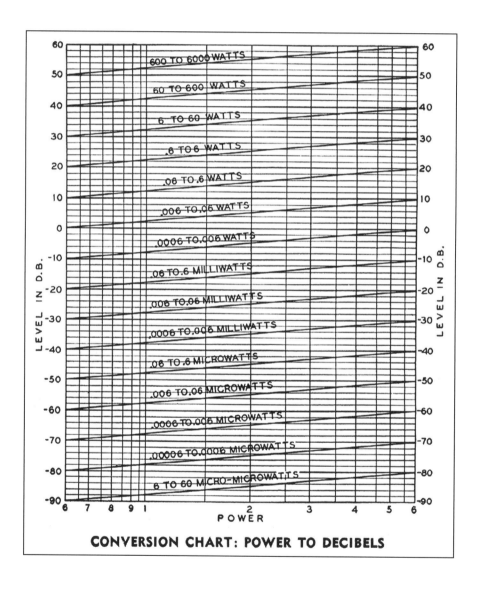

CONVERSION CHART: POWER TO DECIBELS

Transistor Symbols

$C_{b'c}$ collector-to-base feedback capacitance

C_c collector-to-case capacitance

C_{cb} collector-to-base feedback capacitance

C_{ibo} input capacitance, open circuit (common base)

C_{ieo} input capacitance, open circuit (common emitter)

C_{obo} output capacitance, open circuit (common base)

C_{oeo} output capacitance, open circuit (common emitter)

$E_{s/b}$ second-breakdown energy

f_c cutoff frequency

f_{hfb} small-signal forward-current transfer-ratio cutoff frequency, short-circuit (common base)

f_{hfe} small-signal forward-current transfer-ratio cutoff frequency, short-circuit (common emitter)

f_T gain-bandwidth product (frequency at which small-signal forward-current transfer ratio, common emitter, extrapolates to unity)

g_{me} small-signal transconductance (common emitter)

G_{PB} large-signal average power gain (common base)

G_{pb} small-signal average power gain (common base)

G_{PE} large-signal average power gain (common emitter)

G_{pe} small-signal average power gain (common emitter)

h_{FB} static forward-current transfer ratio (common base)

h_{fb} small-signal forward-current transfer ratio, short circuit (common base)

h_{FE} static forward-current transfer ratio (common emitter)

h_{fe} small-signal forward-current transfer ratio, short circuit (common emitter)

h_{ib} small-signal input impedance, short circuit (common base)

h_{IE} static input resistance (common emitter)

h_{ie} small-signal input impedance, short circuit (common emitter)

h_{ob} small-signal output impedance, open circuit (common base)

h_{oe} small-signal output impedance, open circuit (common emitter)

h_{rb} small-signal reverse-voltage transfer ratio, open circuit (common base)

h_{re} small-signal reverse-voltage transfer ratio, open circuit (common emitter)

I_B base current

I_{B1} turn-on current

I_{B2} turn-off current

I_C collector current

i_c collector current, instantaneous value

I_{CB} collector-cutoff current

I_{CBO} collector-cutoff current, emitter open

I_{CEO} — collector-cutoff current, base open

I_{CER} — collector-cutoff current, specified resistance between base and emitter

I_{CES} — collector-cutoff current, base short-circuited to emitter

I_{CEV} — collector-cutoff current, specified voltage between base and emitter

I_{CRX} — collector-cutoff current, specified circuit between base and emitter

I_{CS} — switching current (at minimum h_{FE} per specification)

I_E — emitter current

I_{EBO} — emitter-cutoff current, collector open

$I_{S/b}$ — second-breakdown collector current

MAG — maximum available amplifier gain

MAG_c — maximum available conversion gain

MUG — maximum usable amplifier gain

P_{BE} — total dc or average power input to base (common emitter)

p_{BE} — total instantaneous power input to base (common emitter)

P_{CB} — total dc or average power input to collector (common base)

p_{CB} — total instantaneous power input to collector (common base)

P_{CE} — total dc or average power input to collector (common emitter)

p_{CE} — total instantaneous power input to collector (common emitter)

P — total dc or average power input to emitter (common base)

p_{EB} — total instantaneous power input to emitter (common base)

P_{IB} — large-signal input power (common base)

P_{ib} — small-signal input power (common base)

P_{IE} — large-signal input power (common emitter)

P_{ie} — small-signal input power (common emitter)

P_{ob} — large-signal output power (common base)

P_{ob} — small-signal output power (common base)

P_{OE} — large-signal output power (common emitter)

P_{oe} — small-signal output power (common emitter)

Q_s — stored base charge

$r_{CE}(sat)$ — collector-to-emitter saturation resistance

$Re(h_{ie})$ — real part of small-signal input impedance, short circuit (common emitter)

R_G — generator resistance

R_{ie} — input resistance (common emitter)

R_L — load resistance

R_{oe} — output resistance (common emitter)

R_S — source resistance

V_{BB} — base-supply voltage

V_{BC} — base-to-collector voltage

V_{BE} — base-to-emitter voltage

$V_{(BR)CBO}$ — collector-to-base breakdown voltage, emitter open

$V_{(BR)CEO}$ — collector-to-emitter breakdown voltage, base open

$V_{(BR)CER}$ — collector-to-emitter breakdown voltage, specified resistance between base and emitter

$V_{(BR)CES}$ — collector-to-emitter breakdown voltage, base short-circuited to emitter

$V_{(BR)CEV}$ — collector-to-emitter breakdown voltage, specified voltage between base and emitter

$V_{(BR)EBO}$ — emitter-to-base breakdown voltage, collector open

V_{CB} — collector-to-base voltage

$V_{CB}(fl)$ — dc open-circuit voltage between collector and base (floating potential), emitter biased with respect to base

$V_{CE}(fl)$ — dc open-circuit voltage between collector and emitter (floating potential), base biased with respect to emitter

V_{CBO}	collector - to - base voltage (emitter open)	c_{gd}	gate-to-drain capacitance (includes 0.1-pF interlead capacitance)
V_{CBV}	collector - to - base voltage, specified voltage between emitter and base	c_{gs}	gate - to - source interlead and case capacitance
V_{CC}	collector-supply voltage	C_{iss}	small-signal input capacitance, short circuit
V_{CE}	collector-to-emitter voltage	C_{rss}	small-signal reverse transfer capacitance, short circuit
V_{CEO}	collector-to-emitter voltage, base open	g_{fs}	forward transconductance
V_{CER}	collector - to - emitter voltage, specified resistance between base and emitter	g_{is}	input conductance
		g_{os}	output conductance
V_{CES}	collector - to - emitter voltage, base short-circuited to emitter	I_D	dc drain current
		$I_{DS}(OFF)$	drain-to-source OFF current
V_{CEV}	collector - to - emitter voltage, specified voltage between base and emitter	I_{GSS}	gate leakage current
		NF	spot noise figure (generator resistance $R_G = 1$ megohm)
$V_{CE}(sat)$	collector-to-emitter saturation voltage	r_c	effective gate series resistance
V_{EB}	emitter - to - base voltage,	r_d	active channel resistance
$V_{EB}(fl)$	dc open-circuit voltage between emitter and base (floating potential), collector biased with respect to base	r_d'	unmodulated channel resistance
		$r_{DS}(ON)$	drain-to-source ON resistance
V_{EBO}	emitter - to-base voltage, collector open	r_{gd}	gate-to-drain leakage resistance
V_{EE}	emitter-supply voltage	r_{gs}	gate-to-source leakage resistance
V_{RT}	reach-through voltage	V_{DB}	drain-to-substrate voltage
Y_{fe}	forward transconductance	V_{DS}	drain-to-source voltage
Y_{ie}	input admittance	V_{GB}	dc gate-to-substrate voltage
Y_{oe}	output admittance		
Y_{re}	reverse transconductance	v_{GB}	peak gate-to-subtrate voltage

MOS FIELD-EFFECT TRANSISTOR SYMBOLS

		V_{GS}	dc gate-to-source voltage
A	voltage amplification $(= Y_{fs}/Y_{os} + Y_L)$	v_{GS}	peak gate-to-source voltage
B_{os}	$= C_{ds}$	$V_{GS}(OFF)$	gate-to-source cutoff voltage
c_c	intrinsic channel capacitance	Y_{fs}	forward transadmittance $\approx g_{fs}$
c_{ds}	drain-to-source capacitance (includes approximately 1-pF drain-to-case and interlead capacitance)	Y_{os}	output admittance $= g_{os} + jB_{os}$, $B_{os} = \omega C_{ds}$
		Y_L	load admittance $= g_L + jB_L$

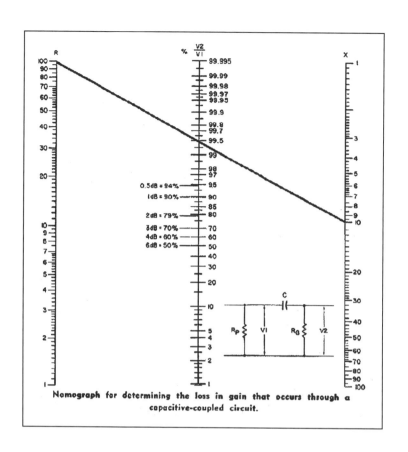

Nomograph for determining the loss in gain that occurs through a capacitive-coupled circuit.

Power Transformer Schematics

Metaltronix
M-1000, M-500, Blues-59

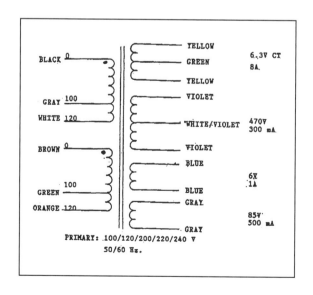

Ampeg, Crate (Stealth), and Lee Jackson Amplifiers

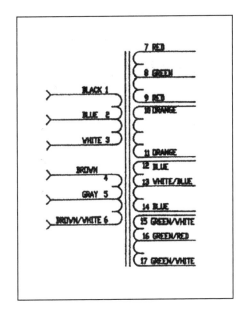

Output Transformer Schematics

Metaltronix
M-1000, M-500, Blues-59

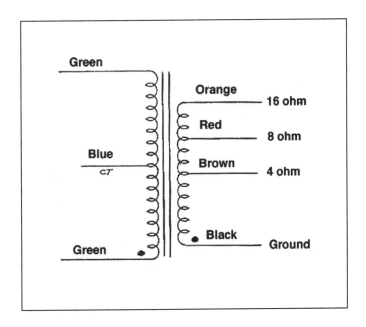

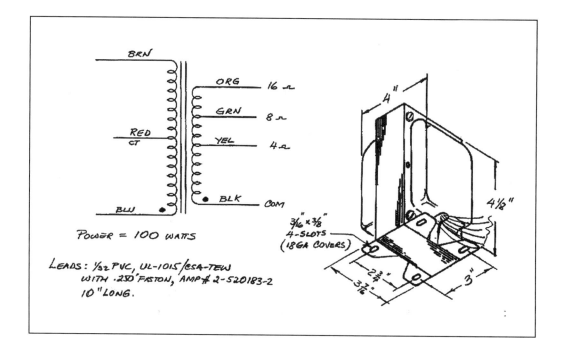

Fender Date Codes

Fender amplifiers made after 1953 have a date code stamped on their tube charts. The first letter stands for the year of manufacture, and the second stands for the month.

First Letter

A	=	1951
B	=	1952
C	=	1953
D	=	1954
E	=	1955
F	=	1956
G	=	1957
H	=	1958
I	=	1959
J	=	1960
K	=	1961
L	=	1962
M	=	1963
N	=	1964
O	=	1965

Second Letter

A	=	January
B	=	February
C	=	March
D	=	April
E	=	May
F	=	June
G	=	July
H	=	August
I	=	September
J	=	October
K	=	November
L	=	December

COMPARISON CHART FOR JENSEN LOUD SPEAKERS
ALNICO 5 PM MODELS

4"	5"	6"	8"	10"	12"	15"	18"	*GAP ENERGY	DESIG-NATION	SERIES
							PP6-18	28.1	J	professional
						PHM-15		19.5	K	professional
								13.6	L	professional
								9.5	M	concert
					P12-N	P15-N		6.6	N	concert
					P12-P	P15-P		4.6	P	concert
			P8-Q	P10-Q	P12-Q	P15-Q		3.2	Q	concert
			P8-R	P10-R	P12-R			2.2	R	concert
			P8-S	P10-S	P12-S			1.5	S	standard
		P6-T	P8-T	P10-T	P12-T			1.1	T	standard
			P8-U					.74	U	standard
	P5-V	P6-V	P8-V					.51	V	standard
								.36	W	standard
P4-X	P5-X	P6-X						.25	X	standard

R series = 1" voice coil
Q series = 1¼" voice coil
P and N series = 1½" voice coil

Marshall Output Transformer Color Code

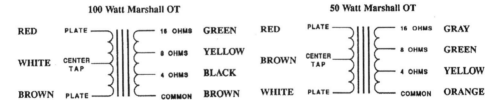

100 Watt Marshall OT

RED — PLATE — 16 OHMS — GREEN
WHITE — CENTER TAP — 8 OHMS — YELLOW
— 4 OHMS — BLACK
BROWN — PLATE — COMMON — BROWN

50 Watt Marshall OT

RED — PLATE — 16 OHMS — GRAY
BROWN — CENTER TAP — 8 OHMS — GREEN
— 4 OHMS — YELLOW
WHITE — PLATE — COMMON — ORANGE

Marshall Serial Numbers

Beginning thru December 1983   SL/A_____ _____ _____

Type & Pwr output   Seriel Number   Date Code (Year Made)

Type & Pwr output

A/ All 200 watt Models   ST/A 100 watt Tremelo
/A All 200 watt Plexi's   ST/ 100 watt tremelo Plexi's
SL/A 100 watt Lead   S/A 50 watt Lead
SL/ 100 watt lead Plexi's   S/ 50 watt JTM Plexi's
SB/A 100 watt Bass   T/A 50 wat tremelo
SB/ 100 watt Bass Plexi's   T/ 50 watt JTM Tremelo Plexi's
SP/ 100 watt P.A

Date Code (year Made)

No Letter: June 30 1969 and earlier
(A) July 1 1969 thru December 31 1970
(C) 1971 (D) 1972 (E) 1973 (F) 1974
(G) 1975 (H) 1976 (J) 1977 (K) 1978
(L) 1979 (M) 1980 (N) 1981 (P) 1982
(R) 1983

From January 1984   S/A _____ _____

All Models   Date Code   Serial Number

Date Code

(S) 1984 (T) 1985 (U) 1986
(V) 1987 (W) 1988 (X) 1989
(Y) 1990 (O) Silver Jubilee

CHAPTER 5
SOLIDSTATE CIRCUITS

This is a collection of solidstate circuit designs that I have used for various situations, such as gain boosters, active splitters to connect multiple amplifiers or effects together, active mixers used to mix multiple effects unit outputs together, or used so a guitar can drive the inputs to multiple effect units. At the end, I have several DC power supply circuits for powering either the various circuits in this book or individual effects pedals.

Solidstate ICs

The IC op-amp has high-input impedance with very low-output impedance. It has two inputs: One is called the *non-inverting* input and the other is the *inverting*. A positive signal applied to the non-inverting input will create a positive output signal; a positive signal applied to the inverting input will create a negative output signal. Because of the high gain of the amplifier, only the smallest signal can be applied to the input of the IC to keep the output clean or undistorted. The high gain of the op-amp will make feedback-controlled circuits very accurate. The gain determined by the op-amp feedback network is from 1 to 100 or more. This is much less than the open-loop gain of the op-amp, which ranges from 100,000 to several million.

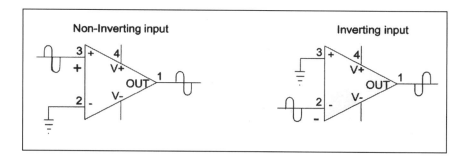

Buffer 1

This circuit can be used to drive long instrument cords, or at the output of an effects pedal that doesn't have a buffered out, such as a Vox Wah-Wah. This circuit is designed to work on a bipolar supply, +V/−V.

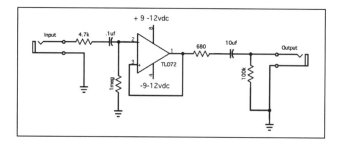

Buffer 2

This is same circuit as the above, but this one will work on a single-supply voltage.

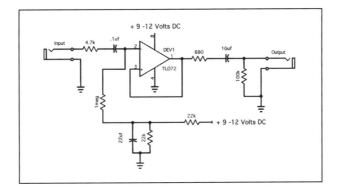

Buffer 3

This is a buffer with adjustable gain. It works well at adding gain to the output of an instrument without adding any coloration to the sound. You can use TLO72 or 4558 if you want an IC with lower current drain for better battery life. This circuit is designed to work on a dual supply, +V/–V.

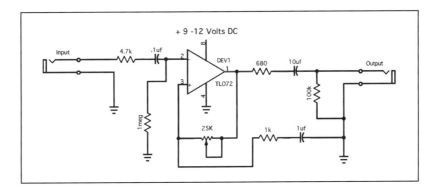

Buffer 4

This is the same circuit as the previous (Buffer 3), except that it works on a single-supply voltage.

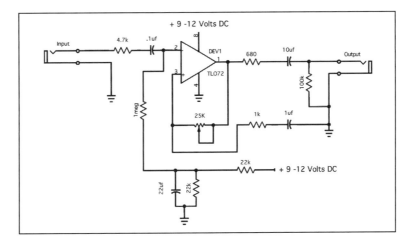

Buffer 5 (Active Splitter)

This buffer is used as an active splitter. Each output is isolated from the other and the input signal. This works great when you want to plug your guitar into two amplifiers. This active "Y" cord keeps the input resistance of the amplifier inputs from loading down your instrument. Because it is a buffer, you can run long cords after the splitter. This circuit is designed to be powered by a dual power supply, +V/–V.

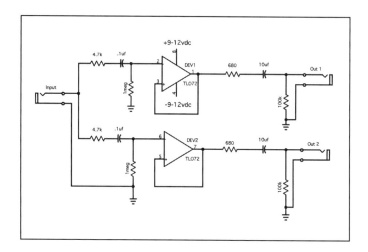

Buffer 6

This is the same circuit as Buffer 5, except that it works on a single-supply voltage.

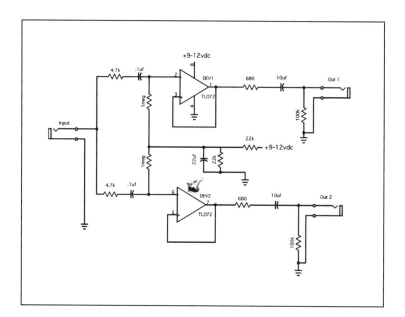

Buffer 7

This is an active buffer with one of its output transformers isolated. This helps when there is a ground problem among several amplifiers or effects. I would suggest using the best one-to-one transformer with the best frequency response that you can find. This circuit was designed to be powered by a dual power supply. If you need a splitter to be powered by a single supply, add the transformer to Buffer 6.

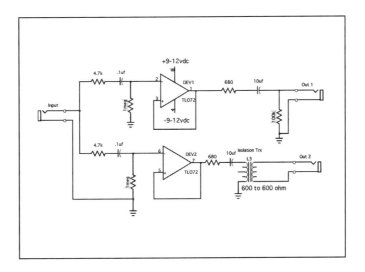

Buffer 8

This circuit is great for driving the input of multiple effects units or driving the inputs of multiple amplifiers. This circuit was designed to be powered by a dual power supply.

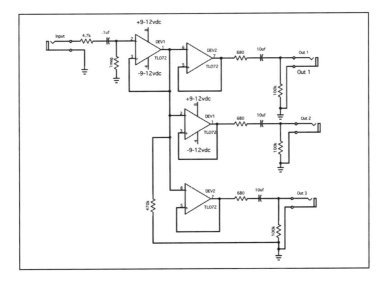

Mixers

These circuits can be used for mixing multiple effects unit outputs to one. You can use two of these circuits for a stereo setup. This works well to mix multiple wireless system outputs to one output, multiple keyboards, etc.

Mixer 1

This mixer is a simple design. It works on a single transistor with low current drain, which means long battery life. It works on a single-supply voltage. Use any PNP transistor of your liking.

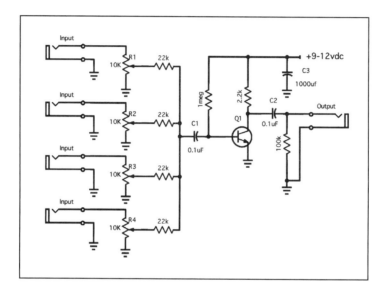

Mixer 2

This is a mixer that uses an op-amp. There is not a lot of isolation between the inputs, and it works on a single supply. It has low current drain and long battery life.

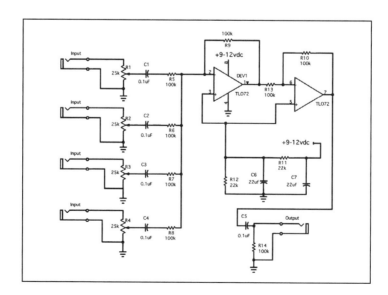

Mixer 3

This mixer circuit has great isolation between the input signals. With high supply lines, it can accept large signals with great headroom. This circuit works on a dual power supply, +V/–V.

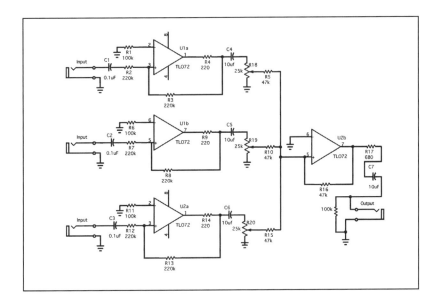

Solidstate Power Supplies

Supply 1

This is a single-voltage power supply. It's good for powering effects pedals. It uses an LM317 adjustable regulator.

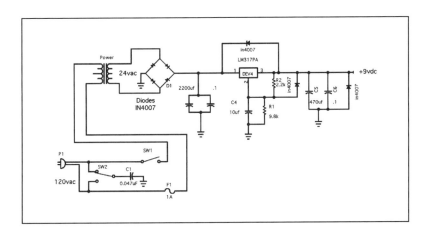

Supply 2

This is a great power supply to power effects pedals that run on 9 V. It uses a standard 8-V regulator to achieve the 9.5 VDC.

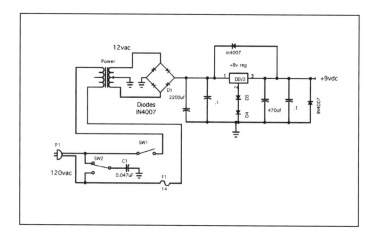

Supply 3

This is a dual-supply 9.5 VDC. It can be used to power the solidstate circuits that need a dual supply.

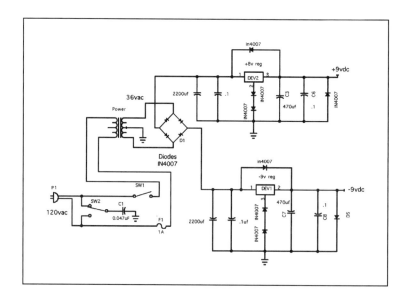

Supply 4

This supply can be used to power switching circuits, effects loops, and solidstate reverbs.

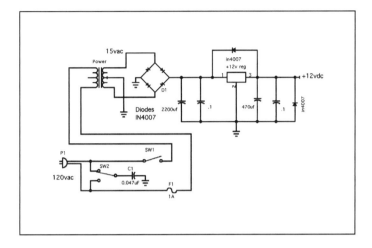

Supply 5

This dual supply can be used for most op-amp circuits and switching circuits.

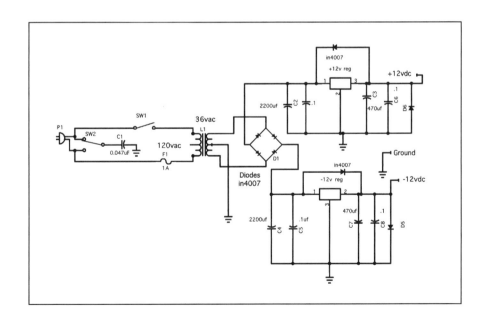

MC7800 Series

THREE-TERMINAL POSITIVE FIXED VOLTAGE REGULATORS

SILICON MONOLITHIC INTEGRATED CIRCUITS

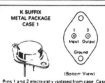

K SUFFIX
METAL PACKAGE
CASE 1

1 2
Input Output
Ground

(Bottom View)

Pins 1 and 2 electrically isolated from case. Case is third electrical connection

T SUFFIX
PLASTIC PACKAGE
CASE 221A

PIN 1 INPUT
2 GROUND
3 OUTPUT

(Heatsink surface connected to Pin 2)

STANDARD APPLICATION

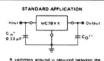

Input — MC78XX — Output
C_{in}^* 0.33 μF C_O^{**}

A common ground is required between the input and the output voltages. The input voltage must remain typically 2.0 V above the output voltage even during the low point on the input ripple voltage.

XX - these two digits of the type number indicate voltage.

* C_{in} is required if regulator is located an appreciable distance from power supply filter.

** C_O is not needed for stability, however, it does improve transient response

XX indicates nominal voltage

MC7900 Series

THREE-TERMINAL NEGATIVE FIXED VOLTAGE REGULATORS

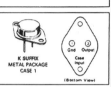

K SUFFIX
METAL PACKAGE
CASE 1

Gnd Output
Case Input

(Bottom View)

T SUFFIX
PLASTIC PACKAGE
CASE 221A

PIN 1 GROUND
2 INPUT
3 OUTPUT

(Heatsink surface connected to Pin 2)

STANDARD APPLICATION

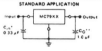

Input — MC79XX — Output
C_{in}^* 0.33 μF C_O^{**} 1.0 μF

A common ground is required between the input and the output voltages. The input voltage must remain typically 2.0 V more negative even during the high point on the input ripple voltage.

XX - these two digits of the type number indicate voltage.

* C_{in} is required if regulator is located an appreciable distance from power supply filter.

** C_O improves stability and transient response.

LM117 LM217 LM317

THREE-TERMINAL ADJUSTABLE POSITIVE VOLTAGE REGULATORS

SILICON MONOLITHIC INTEGRATED CIRCUIT

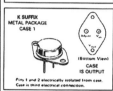

K SUFFIX
METAL PACKAGE
CASE 1

Adjust V_{in}

(Bottom View)

CASE IS OUTPUT

Pins 1 and 2 electrically isolated from case. Case is third electrical connection.

T SUFFIX
PLASTIC PACKAGE
CASE 221A

PIN 1. ADJUST
2. V_{out}
3. V_{in}

Heatsink surface connected to Pin 2

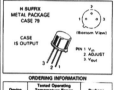

H SUFFIX
METAL PACKAGE
CASE 79

(Bottom View)

CASE IS OUTPUT

PIN 1 V_{in}
2. ADJUST
3. V_{out}

ORDERING INFORMATION

Device	Tested Operating Temperature Range	Package
LM117H LM117K	$T_J = -55°C$ to $+150°C$	Metal Can Metal Power
LM217H LM217K	$T_J = -25°C$ to $+150°C$	Metal Can Metal Power
LM317H LM317K LM317T	$T_J = 0°C$ to $+125°C$	Metal Can Metal Power Plastic Power
LM317BT#	$T_J = -40°C$ to $+125°C$	Plastic Power

#Automotive temperature range selections are available with special test conditions and additional tests. Contact your local Motorola sales office for information.

LM150 LM250 LM350

THREE-TERMINAL ADJUSTABLE POSITIVE VOLTAGE REGULATORS

SILICON MONOLITHIC INTEGRATED CIRCUIT

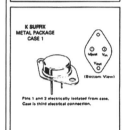

K SUFFIX
METAL PACKAGE
CASE 1

Adjust V_{in}
V_{out}

(Bottom View)

Pins 1 and 2 electrically isolated from case. Case is third electrical connection.

T SUFFIX
PLASTIC PACKAGE
CASE 221A

PIN 1. ADJUST
2. V_{out}
3. V_{in}

Heatsink surface connected to Pin 2

ORDERING INFORMATION

Device	Tested Operating Temperature Range	Package
LM150K	$T_J = -55°C$ to $+150°C$	Metal Power
LM250K	$T_J = -25°C$ to $+150°C$	
LM350K	$T_J = 0°C$ to $+125°C$	Plastic Power
LM350T		
LM350BT#	$T_J = -40°C$ to $+125°C$	

Chapter 6
Amplifier Modifications

Amplifiers are basically designed in blocks. These blocks are made of different gain stages. They consist of tone circuits, distortion generators, effects loops, reverb drivers and returns, and a power amp section. This chapter on modifying amps will cover the different gain stages (or blocks) and will give you an idea of the various available options so you can achieve the best tone for your playing style.

Some Background on Fender Amps

Leo Fender was a practical man who built amplifiers using quality parts. The amps were simple in design and very reliable—great starting points for modifications. The fibreboard circuit cards made it easy to replace and add parts. When I was working for Fender, we were still using these circuit cards. When you wanted to change a layout, all you had to do was cut a piece of fibreboard to the size you needed, place the eyelets where you wanted to mount the resistors and capacitors, and assemble. This is different than having to do a printed circuitboard (a.k.a. PCB) layout either by hand (called a *tape up*) or computer (via CAD software), and then sending your designs to a circuitboard house, and waiting for weeks to get your boards back—only to find out that you put a part in the wrong place.

Fibreboards still have their drawbacks—their assembly is slow, and they cannot be auto-inserted. Fibreboards are also extremely susceptible to climate changes. Because Fenders were assembled in California—which is basically a desert—crackling and popping sounds were only an issue for the amps that were shipped to more humid environments. People would call complaining that their amplifiers made noise. They would send the amplifiers back, only to find that they worked fine in California because of its humidity-free climate. This problem would get worse as an amplifier would age because the fibreboard would begin to absorb moisture.

Fender basically set the industry standard for musical amplifiers. The first of anything is always the one that demands comparison. And speaking of comparison, Jim Marshall was one of the most famous Fender imitators. Ken Bran, who worked for Jim, copied an early Fender Bassman, and the only differences between the two amps were the output tubes. The reason for this difference was that the Mullard EL-34 was a lot cheaper in England than the American 6L6. They flipped over the chassis so the tubes pointed up—which also caused the input jacks to be at the opposite end of the amplifier compared to the Fender amps. The early Marshalls also used a hard fibreboard circuit card. The only difference was that the components were mounted on stand-offs with point-to-point wiring. Marshalls moved on to fiberglass circuitboards long before Fender did. While I was at Fender, one of the head designers named Ed Johns fought tooth and nail to keep fibreboards, constantly proving their better isolation properties. He had to step up his efforts when CBS bought Fender. They tried to streamline everything—including the amplifier lines. Quicker assembly and cheaper manufacturing costs were eventually the end of CBS.

As music and playing styles changed, Fender and Marshall didn't move at the same speeds in terms of new amplifier designs. This opened the door for new companies to enter the arena. I, too, left Fender in 1983 to open Metaltronix because I wanted to supply amplifiers that Fender wasn't building. There was a void in the market that the two companies didn't see.

You will find that most amplifiers on the market are designed around either the Fender or Marshall layout; the manufacturers mix-and-match different gain blocks, increasing and decreasing gain, and adding features the market dictates. In this chapter, I'll give you the building blocks for mixing and matching so you can build your own version of the next killer amp. I'll start with tube gain stages, move on to tone circuits, and then talk about buffers and other topics.

So get your soldering iron and let's go!

Gain Stages

One of the most popular gain stages is the *common cathode*—the signal is applied to the grid, the output is taken from the plate, and the cathode is tied to ground. Resistance coupling is one of the most widely used methods of coupling vacuum tubes. They are simplistic in design and construction, have a wide frequency range, and can be manufactured at a low cost. When applying a sine wave signal to the control grid, the voltage at the plate will rise and fall in accordance with the signal at the grid and will be 180 degrees out of phase. If the tube is not driven into overload, the signal at the plate will be an inversion of the signal voltage at the grid, but of a greater magnitude depending on the amplification factor of the tube. As a rule, resistance-coupled amplifiers are designed to use self-bias. To obtain a large voltage gain in a resistance-coupled gain stage, the plate-load resistor must have as large a value as is practical. The higher the value of the plate-load resistance, the greater the DC voltage drop across it, and the lower the actual voltage at the plate of the tube. There is a limit to the value of the load resistance. The DC voltage drop across the plate-load resistor must be subtracted from the supply voltage (B+) to arrive at the actual value of the voltage at the plate of the tube. If the value of the load resistor is high, only a small portion of the supply voltage will be available at the plate—this might be too low for proper operation. Under the best conditions, only 80 percent of the tube amplification can be attained. After a certain value of resistance has been reached, the gain will increase very slowly and never reach the full amplification factor of the tube.

A loss of gain in the lower frequencies is caused by the high reactance of the coupling capacitor. At lower frequencies, the plate resistance appears across the series combination of the coupling capacitor and the grid resistor, which is applied to the input of the following stage. The best low frequency response is obtained when the coupling capacitor is large in value, so that its reactance is negligible at the lowest amplification frequency. The high frequency response falls off because of the interelectrode capacitance of the tube, as well as the distributed capacitance of the tube socket and the associated wiring. These capacities are shunt with the plate and control grid circuit and act as a low-impedance path to ground at the higher frequencies. When the reactance of the coupling capacitor at the lower frequencies becomes equal to the grid resistor, the frequency response will be 3 dB down. When you are designing a capacitive-coupled circuit, it is useful to be able to predict what proportion of the voltage across the plate resistor will appear across the grid resistor.

The cathode capacitor size is selected for a value that will have a reactance of 1/10th the resistance of the cathode resistor. Practical sizes are from 22 to 50 uF. The purpose of the cathode capacitor is to provide a low-impedance path for the signal voltage to ground and to remove it from the cathode resistor. As the size of the cathode bypass capacitor is reduced, negative current feedback is increased. If this capacitor is made smaller, the gain will begin to fall to the lower frequencies and the higher frequency characteristics will start to rise. A small capacitor across the cathode resistor is often used to increase the high-frequency response.

Common Cathode Gain Chart

V+	Plate V_A	R1 $R_A (\Omega)$	R2 $R_X (\Omega)$	I_A	V_{OUT}(pp)	Gain A_V
150 V	104 V	475 K	10 K	97 μA	40 V	13.3
150 V	75 V	475 K	1 K	158 μA	62 V	20.7
150 V	137 V	100 K	10 K	130 μA	16 V	5.3
150 V	127 V	100 K	1 K	230 μA	32 V	10.7
150 V	75 V	100 K	470	750 μA	20 V	30.7
300 V	208 V	475 K	10 K	194 μA	74 V	14.8
300 V	150 V	475 K	1 K	316 μA	120 V	26.0
300 V	275 V	100 K	10 K	250 μA	32 V	5.8
300 V	254 V	100 K	1 K	460 μA	74 V	11.3
300 V	150 V	100 K	470	1 m 5	40 V	32.0

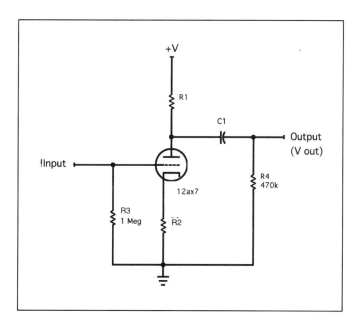

Gain 1

This is a classic Fender-style common cathode gain stage. The 25-uF capacitor bypasses the 1.5-K cathode resistor to produce a 5-Hz gain increase.

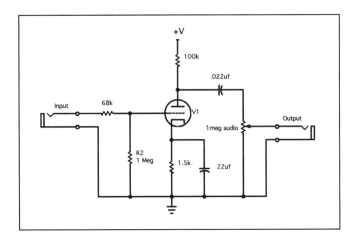

Gain 2

This is a standard Marshall gain stage C2, which adds a high mid boost.

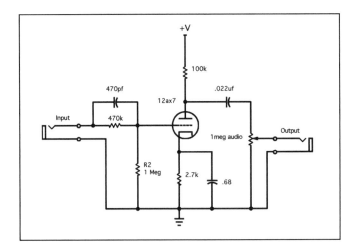

Tone Stages

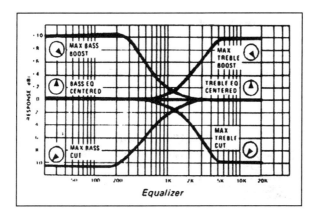

Equalizer

A *tone control* is a variable filter that has one or more adjustable elements with which the user may vary the frequency response of an amplifier to suit his (or her) taste. The tone control(s) usually consist of a resistance capacitance network in which the resistance is the variable element. These circuits are also known as *degenerative amplifier equalizers*, and employ reactive components in the cathode and plate circuits of a tube. The amount of equalization is controlled by the potentiometers, which control the degeneration in the cathode circuit. Because the amount of equalization affects the gain of the amplifier stage, the main gain control of the amplifier must be changed to compensate for every change in the amount of equalization.

Here is a collection of tone circuits that you can use in various positions. Each has its own unique sound and curve characteristic.

Tone 1

Here is a simple, one-knob tone circuit. As you rotate the control in one direction, it cuts the bass frequency, and as you turn it the opposite direction, it cuts the higher frequencies.

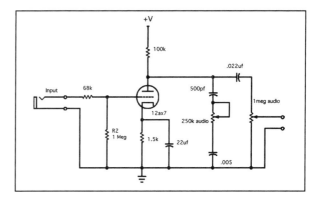

Tone 2

This tone circuit is a lot like the previous one, except for the addition of high- and low-end boost.

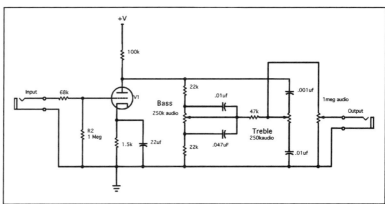

Tone 3

Here is a little twist to the last one.

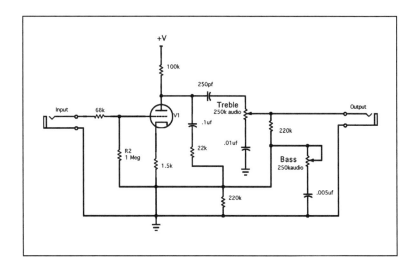

Tone 4

This tone circuit was used on very early Fender Bassman amplifiers. You can bring your feedback to this circuit to have a presence control close to the rest of the tone controls. Because of the feedback, it should be close to the last stage before the power amp stage.

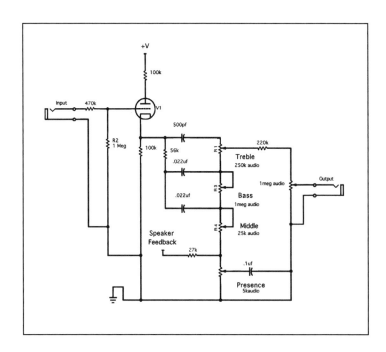

Tone 5

This is the classic Fender clean-tone circuit. It can be used in multiple places in the gain stage blocks.

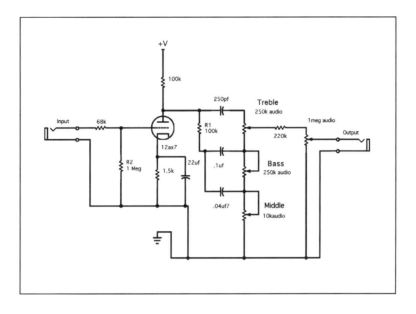

Tone 6

This is a classic Marshall tone circuit and is a cathode follower. The output impedance is lower than the classic Fender (Tone 5).

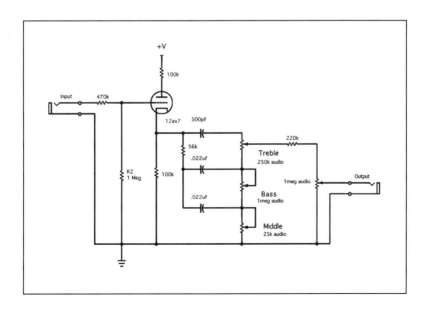

Tone 7

This is more of a resonator circuit than a tone circuit; it should be the last stage in line before the power (phase inverter) stage. This circuit allows you to have a presence control without compromising the feedback loop.

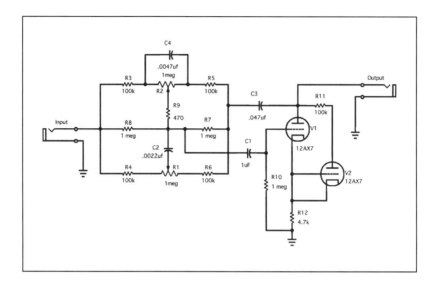

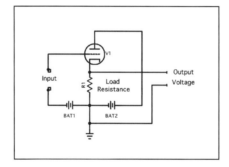

Tube Buffers

The buffer takes advantage of all of the properties of the cathode follower circuit. The high-input impedance of the buffer does not load the preamp output. The output impedance of the cathode follower is low and will drive any effects unit or long guitar cords without frequency loss. Although the cathode follower gives no voltage gain, it is an effective amplifier in instances where one would want to drive a low-impedance load, or drive a load of varying impedance with a signal that has good regulation. The cathode follower is one of the most linear tube circuits; the output signal will be a highly accurate copy of the input signal. The primary reason for using a buffer is that the cathode follower input impedance is so high that little or no load is placed on the preceding circuitry.

Buffer 1

This is a really good buffer. It is a *self-biasing* cathode follower, which means that the tube itself determines its operating point. The circuit is shown using a 12AX7a. This tube will work fine, but if you want the buffer to have better current capability use a 12AT7. The 12AT7 has a high power rating, which allows higher signal levels while retaining low impedances.

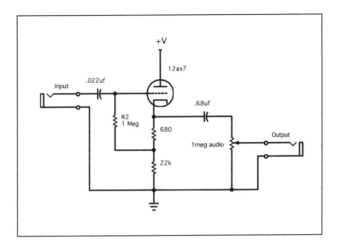

Buffer 2

This buffer is a cathode follower with an active, constant-current source output. The hum rejection of the active current source is 10 dB better than that of the resistive load. This buffer will pass 80 Vpp, which is more headroom than needed for guitar signal; it is also quite *transparent*—keeping more of the natural instrument sound.

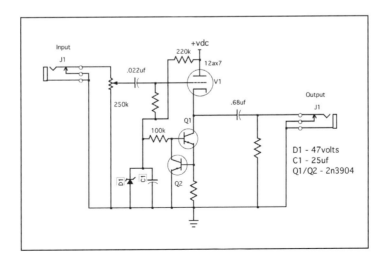

Effects

Most effects loops are between the preamp and power amp sections of an amplifier. Early amplifiers didn't have effects loops, which forced the player to place his floor effects between the guitar and the input of his amplifier. Whereas this worked fine for some effects such as wah-wahs and fuzz boxes, it didn't produce the effect that the player was creating in the studio. With the introduction of the effects loop, the player could now put his delay, chorus, or reverb after the preamp section of his amplifier; this would give him a closer sound to what he was hearing in the studio. Harmonics and overtones that were produced by the preamp stages were enhanced by the effects that were plugged into the loop. Some of the earliest loops where just 1/4" jacks that where placed between the preamp and power amp sections without any other circuitry. This caused problems with older effects units and the lengths of the cords being used, and caused impedance mismatching of the internal stages of the amplifier; these mismatches would cause the amplifiers to loose gain and sound dull or muffled. To fix this, it was discovered that the amplifier needed a buffered output; this kept the effect or guitar from loading down the preamp stage of the amplifier. Because most effects units had buffered outputs, it wasn't mandatory to have a return buffer. With the increase in preamp output and professional rack gear, the need for adjustable effects loops became more and more evident. These allow the player to set the amplifier for its optimum sound, and then to be able to match this with the levels of the effects unit, giving the best signal-to-noise ratio.

Effects Loop 1

This is a great effects loop with individual send and return level controls. It can accept large signal swings and is pretty transparent to the original signal. In the circuit below, you must use a switching circuit to switch in and out of the whole circuit (e.g., Switch 5). Because of the gain in the return stage, you can use the loop for a gain boost. On my earlier amplifiers, Paul Gilbert would use the loop as a gain boost for solos.

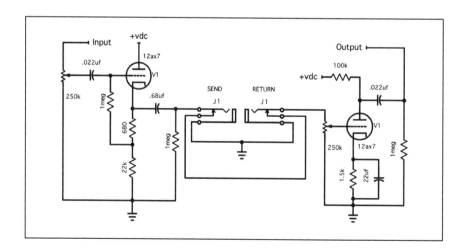

Effects Loop 2

This effects loop circuit allows the original signal to be blended or mixed with the affected signal from the loop. This circuit also needs a switching circuit to switch it in and out of the amplifier's signal path (e.g., Switch 5). Use the return level control to set the amount of effect level to dry signal.

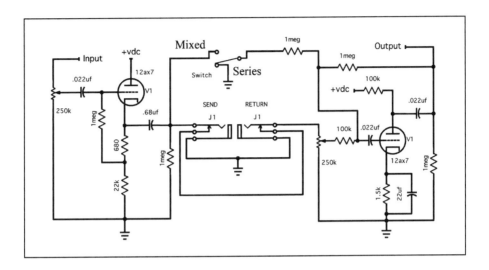

Reverbs

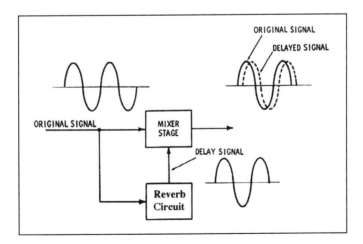

Reverberation is a very popular effect. Most recordings use reverb and most amplifiers today include reverb circuits. The reverberation effect is a combination of a delayed signal that is changing in phase and the original dry signal. If one signal starts out and is followed a fraction of a second later by a second signal just like it, the second signal is lagging in time and phase in reference to the first signal; this is the same effect as if you were to yell in a hallway or canyon. First you hear your voice, and then you hear a copy of your voice— which has bounced off a hall or canyon wall—a fraction of a second later. Some characteristics of sound are determined by the sound source while others are set by the environment. The original will have a timbre composed of a fundamental frequency and specific harmonic overtones with relative amplitudes set by the source. Two sources may have the same frequency components but in different proportions, yielding distinguishable timbres. Each frequency loses energy at varying rates; how these rates combine depends on the source. The environment can alter the spectral balance of the sound in many ways. Some materials are reflective and some are absorptive. Each material in the environment affects the sound—they can cause some frequencies to be diminished in amplitude, while others are increased. The phase shift occurs in the time domain, as the reflected sound waves arrive slightly after any direct sound. The sum of the reflection and the original signal is called *ambience*. Closely spaced, random, non-distinct reflections are called *reverberations*.

Most amplifier reverberation units use a mechanical delay line. This looks like a pair of springs mounted in a box. A transducer is mounted at one end, and a pickup or microphone is mounted on the other end. The transducer turns the audio signal into mechanical vibrations that travel the length of the two springs at slightly different rates due to the way the springs are wound and their lengths. Then the pickup receives the mechanical vibrations from the springs that are delayed and phase shifted. This signal is combined with the original dry signal through a mixer circuit.

Reverb pans are especially prone to picking up radiated noise. A small amount of shielding can keep induced noise to a minimum. Integrated reverb units can be seen as onboard effects.

Reverb 1

This is a standard Fender-style reverb circuit. You would place this circuit after the preamp sections. Generally the return stage is fed into a mixer stage before the power amp section. The reverb driver transformer output impedance is around 8 ohms, which drives the reverb pan input. The reverb pan output is about 2200 ohms. The older style Fenders with this reverb circuit did not have R3 (220 K) and C3 (.0022 uF); this stabilizes the input and adds a smoother sound to the reverb.

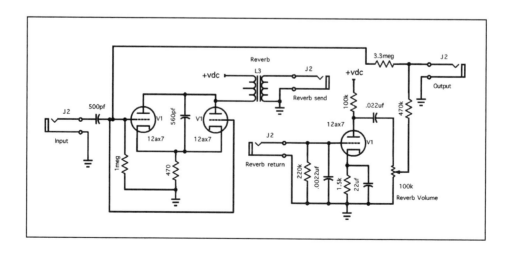

Reverb 2

This circuit is called a *foldback reverb*, is the easiest to install and the least used. I've seen it on several very old Fenders and really inexpensive practice amplifiers. The input of the reverb pan is connected to the output of the output section (speaker); R6 sets the signal level to the pan. This varies depending on the output of the amplifier so that you don't distort the reverb pan. This circuit works well—it can add reverb to an amplifier with little modification, and can be used on amplifiers where space is a consideration.

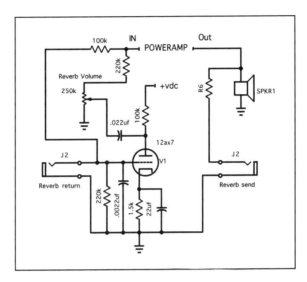

Reverb 3

This reverb return circuit is more of a mixer. The advantage of this mixer is that the two signals are isolated without using feedback. The input impedances are high, so there are no loading considerations on the sources. Each side of the mixer can operate at high gain allowing the return amp to exhibit less gain. This return mixer can be used with both the Reverb 1 and Reverb 2 circuits.

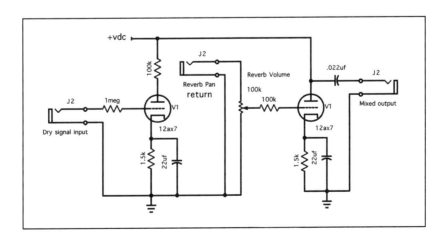

Reverb 4

This is another simple reverb circuit. You need only one tube for both the send and return circuits. This will work with either a 12AX7 or 12AT7 tube.

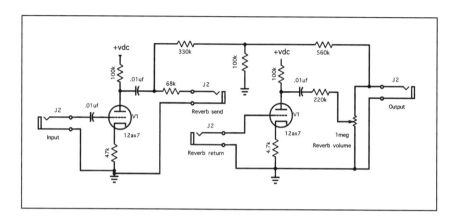

Reverb 5

This is a really great reverb circuit. It allows you to add reverb to your amplifier without having to add a mixer stage between the preamp and power amp. Because of the natural phase properties of the reverb pan, you will not have any problems returning to the phase inverter. To make the circuit simpler, you can use the Reverb 2 drive circuit and then return the reverb signal with this circuit.

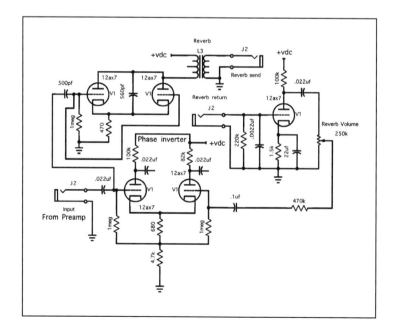

Reverb 6

This is the same circuit as Reverb 5, but with a solidstate reverb drive and a return circuit added—these make it even easier to install. All you need is an op amp (5532) and a reverb pan.

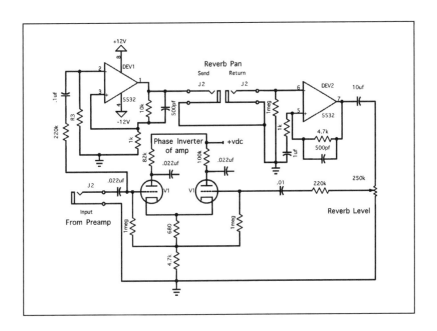

Phase Inverters

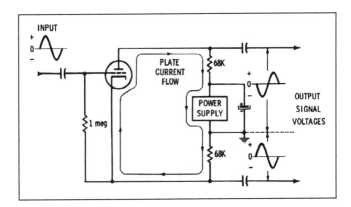

The circuit above is used to provide resistance coupling between the output of a signal tube stage and the input of a push-pull output stage. The necessity for a phase inverter arises because the signal (voltage) inputs to the grids of a push-pull stage must be 180 degrees out of phase and approximately equal in amplitude with respect to each other. These signals are also known as *paraphase signals*.

When the signal (voltage) input to a push-pull stage swings the grid of one tube in a positive direction, it swings the grid of the other tube in a negative direction by a similar amount. With transformer inverters, the transformer couples between stages of the input signal (voltage) to the out-of-phase push-pull stage. This is supplied by means of the center-tapped transformer secondary. Transformer inverters are seldom found in guitar amplifiers, except for some amps from the 1940s and some Fenders from the 1970s. Transformers cost a lot more than tube inverters, and they are more susceptible to pickup hum, so this will be the last time you will hear about transformer inverters in this book.

Phase 1

This is one of the earliest phase inverters; it is also called the *Concertina splitter*. Both the plate and the cathode have identical current output. Both outputs move in unison in relation to each other. The output signal (current) is unity gain to the input because of the cathode follower output. This inverter has a low drive current which makes it impossible to drive high power output stages; it allows AB operation of one device. Its distortion is asymmetrical.

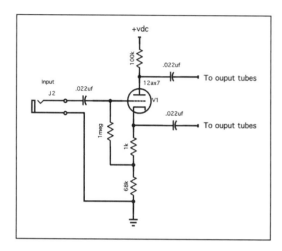

Phase 2

This inverter came about in the 1940s after Bell Labs patented the error-correcting feedback, which applied feedback around the circuit. This phase inverter has a more predictable performance, with one tube providing voltage (current) gain between the input and the power output stage. The second tube, which is an inverter, provides no voltage gain, but because of the feedback it can assure balanced drive of both outputs. This inverter has a higher drive than the Concertina, so it meets the requirements to drive a triode power amp.

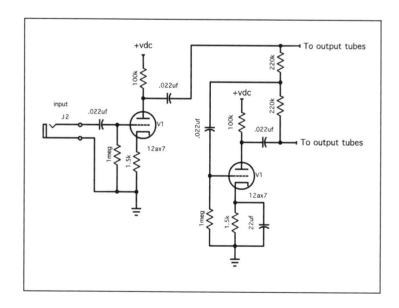

Phase 3

This phase inverter is known as a *Schmidt splitter*. This differential splitter came about because of the long tailed pair; it requires only one input signal to produce balanced outputs.

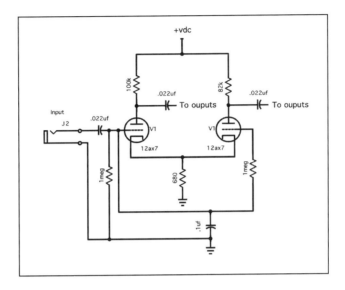

Phase 4

This a Schmidt splitter with a direct-coupled gain stage. The plate of the common cathode gain stage is connected to the input grid of the Schmidt splitter. This architecture allows greater stability in amplifiers with feedback. Phase shift at higher frequencies is low, and I have seen these inverters with the feedback of the amplifier tied to the cathode of the input stage.

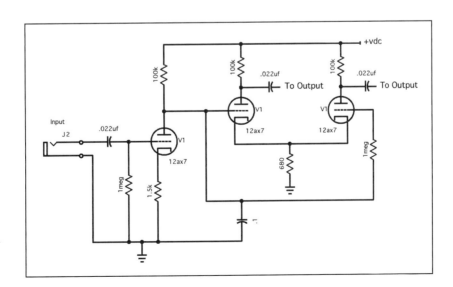

Phase 5

This is a *differential input splitter*. Since the differential amp has high gain, it can easily amplify input signal to drive signal levels. Both outputs have the same drive potential, even though the input signals are not symmetrical. As long as one is the true input, the other is a sample of the output signal. This makes it appropriate to make the feedback look like the input signal.

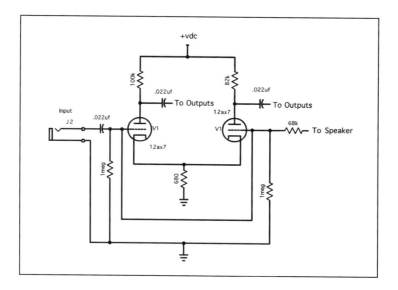

Phase 6

This inverter is a stacked current source, differential amplifier. The complete circuit is then floated on R7, which is made large to provide a constant current. With this, input coupling caps are mandatory. This phase inverter is more suited for guitars because, when pushed, it has a more pleasing distortion with more even harmonics. The more the differential amplifier is balanced the less harmonic distortion results.

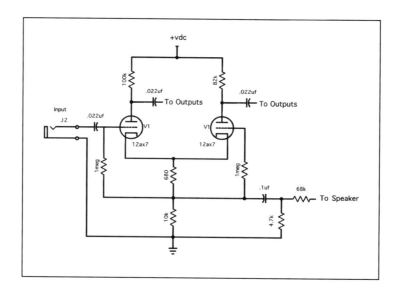

Phase 7

This is a standard Fender phase inverter they started using in the 1960s.

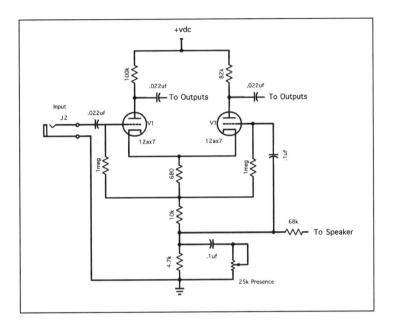

Phase 8

This is the standard Marshall phase inverter. Marshall has kept their resistor and capacitor values pretty much the same throughout their amp line. You will find that most amplifier companies use a combination of both Fender and Marshall components; both companies have found that the plate resistors R3 and R4 set up how much third-order harmonic distortion is present in the output. The more the plate resistors are parallel, the less that third-order harmonic distortion is present. Both of these inverters exceed the frequency range of the guitar, output transformer, or speaker. Guitars go to 10 KHz with harmonics, and guitar speakers have a drastic roll off after 7 KHz—this is why most presence controls are placed in the 7 KHz range, as this gives an amp a shimmery or glassy top end when turned up. Changing the C5 capacitor value shifts the gain response curve up and down the frequency range, and all outputs stay equal in level. The presence control accentuates the upper mid range, which is where the guitar and the human voice both "live." So, by rotating the presence control, you can make your guitar seem more "present" or "upfront." R6 sets up the feedback gain so that you can alter the overall feel of the amp. The more feedback (i.e., a lower resistor value) you have, the tighter the amp sounds, whereas less feedback (i.e., a higher resistor value) loosens the feel and increases the wide band gain. Generally, the tighter settings are good for a clean guitar sound, or if you are playing very loudly, these same settings lack for a distorted guitar sound. This also holds true on the other end. When you loosen the amp's feedback, the distortion sounds better, but the clean sound suffers.

Also, with decreased feedback, the presence control becomes less active. Most companies try to strike a happy medium. You can also add low-end response in the feedback loop by adding a capacitor in line with the feedback (R6) resistor; some call this a *resonance control.*

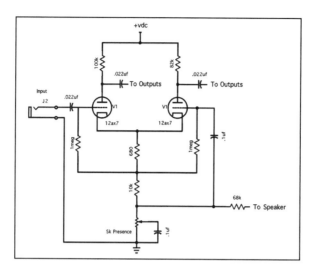

Power Amps

Power amplifiers are of simple design. Their primary function is to take a relatively low signal from a preamp section and provide power to drive a speaker. Most power amps follow one of two designs, with the only difference being the front-end drive circuitry. Power amps work in different classes: The class of an amplifier refers to how the output tubes are biased, and the point on the tube transfer function to which the tube is biased. The class of operation determines the method used to derive the bias setting. There are multiple methods found in guitar power amps, but we will deal with just two of the most popular designs.

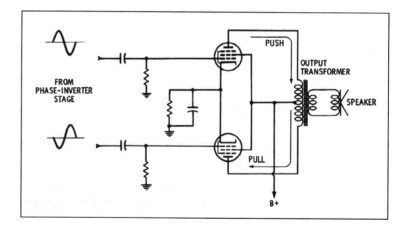

The output transformer is the heart of the tube power amplifier. The way the output tubes are connected to the transformer determines the fundamental character of the circuit. There are two types: single-ended and double-ended. A single tube can drive only one end, with the other end tied to a power supply. Two tubes can each drive each end of the primary windings of an output transformer, requiring a center tap for the B+ supply connection. You can get more power than a single tube can handle and increased efficiency. The idea of an efficient power amp is to get the most current to flow in the output transformer primary. This is done by what is called a *push-pull stage:* One tube pushes current downward through the winding, while the other tube pulls. The output tubes are fed signal voltages so that their grids are 180 degrees out of phase. Because the plates follow the grids, plate current rises in one tube and falls in the other at the same time. By using a push-pull output circuit, more than double the power output is obtained out of one tube. Because the plate current of each tube flows through the same primary windings, there is an increase in efficiency. Once the positive extent of the signal to the first tube has been reached, the drive signal begins to diminish to zero. During the second quarter of the waveform, the second tube drive signal is also diminishing to zero, but from the opposite direction. The first tube conducts *less* current while the second tube begins to conduct *more* current. The fly-back energy from the second end of the primary winding is released to the load, with a small amount bled off by the second tube. The fly-back energy from the transformer is stored as magnetic energy (the electrical energy is transmitted through the movement of electrons that are converted to magnetic energy). Any change in electron flow is resisted by magnetic forces. The initial injection of current is resisted by a magnetic field that induces a current in the opposite direction. When the original current decreases, the transformer creates a magnetic field that induces a reinforcing current. Any variation in current flow causes a change in the induced magnetic field and a reversal in the reactive, magnetically induced current.

Classes of Operation

Class A

In a Class A amplifier, a tube is used to reproduce grid voltage variations across an impedance or a resistance in the plate circuit. These variations are essentially of the same form as the input signal voltage impressed on the grid, but their amplitudes are increased. This increase is accomplished by the operation of the tube at a suitable grid bias so that the grid voltage produces plate current variations proportional to the signal swings. Because the voltage variation obtained in the plate circuit is much larger than that required to swing the grid, amplification of the signal is obtained. Class A operation is typically characterized as the mode of operation where the tube is used only on the linear portion of its transfer function, and all of the tubes are on for 360 degrees of the signal waveform; this mode also produces even harmonic distortion. The transfer function of the tube controls the net transfer function of the power amplifier. At the extremes of the function, the transfer curve is curved. In the middle of the transfer, the curve is linear. If a bias current is selected half-way along this linear portion of the curve, this will keep the signal excursion from exceeding the linear limits, which makes lower distortion possible.

Class AB

A Class AB amplifier employs two tubes connected in a push-pull configuration with a higher negative grid bias than would be used in a Class A stage. With this higher negative bias, the plate and the screen grid voltages can usually be made higher than for Class A amplifiers because the increased negative bias holds the plate current within the limit of the tube plate dissipation rating. As a result of these higher voltages, more power output can be obtained.

Class AB amplifiers are subdivided into Class AB1 and Class AB2. In Class AB1, there is no flow of grid current. The peak signal voltage applied to each grid is not greater than the negative grid bias voltage. Each of the grids, therefore, is not driven to a positive potential and does not draw current.

In Class AB2, the peak signal voltage is greater than the bias so that the grids are driven positive and draw current. Because of the flow of grid current in a Class AB2 stage, there is a loss of power in the grid circuit. The driver stage should be capable of a power output considerably larger than this required power so that distortion introduced in the grid circuit is kept low. Because of the large fluctuations of the plate current in a Class AB2 stage, it is important that the plate power supply has good regulation. In Class AB1, a single pair of 6550a power tubes will provide 100 watts output, whereas in Class AB2, it is possible to achieve 150 watts, but at ten times the THD. Most guitar amplifiers are Class AB2.

Class B

A Class B amplifier uses two tubes connected in push-pull configuration, so biased that the plate current is almost zero when no signal voltage is applied to the grids. Because of this low value of no signal plate current, Class B amplification has the same advantage as Class AB2: Large power output can be obtained without excessive plate dissipation. Class B operation differs from Class AB2 in that plate current is cut off for a larger portion of the negative grid swing, and the signal swing is usually larger than in Class AB2 operation. Because certain triodes used as Class B amplifiers are designed to operate very close to zero bias, the grid of each tube is at a positive potential during all or most of the positive half cycle of its signal swing. In this type of triode operation, considerable grid current is drawn and there is a loss of power in the grid circuit. This condition imposes the same requirement in the driver stage as in a Class AB2 stage. The driver circuit should be capable of delivering considerably more power output than the power required for the grid circuit of the Class B amplifier so that distortion will be low. Because of the high dissipation involved in Class B operation at zero bias, it is not feasible to use tetrodes or pentodes in this type of operation. Determination of load resistance, plate dissipation, power output, and distortion is similar to that for a Class AB2 amplifier. Power amplifier tubes designed for Class A operation can be used in Class AB2 and Class B.

Outputs

Output Mod 1

This modification can warm up the sound of an amplifier that uses an ultralinear output stage. Some of the early '70s Fender amplifiers used ultralinear outputs. These amplifiers had outputs of 135 watts, but were very sterile in sound. This mod will warm up the outputs by making two of the tubes run in triode operation.

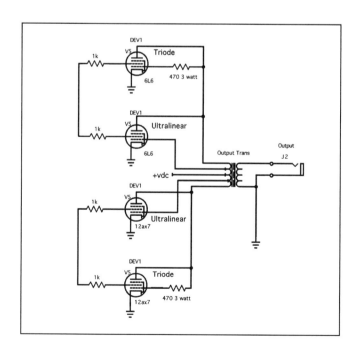

Output Mod 2 (Triode-Pentode Switch)

This is a *half-power* or *triode-pentode switch*. What this circuit does is change the operating mode of the output tubes. Most guitar amplifiers are normally run in the pentode mode with the screens of output tubes tied to the B+ power supply. In triode mode the screens are tied to the plates of the output tubes. To do this mod, all you need is a DPDT switch and some wire. It's important to use a large switch with contact ratings of at least 240 VAC because the switch will see voltages of over 450 VDC. The triode mode has more of a high-frequency roll-off that makes the amp sound smoother at lower volumes. For amplifiers with multiple output tubes, the screen resistors are already tied together, so all you have to do is connect the output tube pair(s) to the switch. Also, if you would like to try something different, you can mix the tube modes, leaving one pair permanently pentode and switching the second pair from pentode to triode.

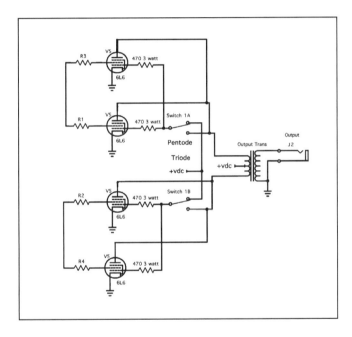

Output Mod 3

This mod helps to suppress output tube spikes and keeps your output transformer from failing when an output tube blows. Generally, it is good practice to replace the diodes after the failure of an output tube, to maintain protection.

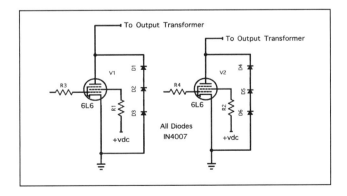

Feedback Circuits

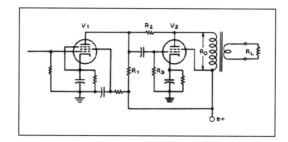

It is possible to modify the characteristics of an amplifier by feeding back a portion of the output to the input. All components, circuits, and tubes included between the point where the feedback is taken off and the point where the feedback energy is inserted are said to be included within a *feedback loop*. An amplifier containing a feedback loop is said to be a *feedback amplifier*. Multiple stages may be included within a feedback loop. The gain and phase shift are functions of frequency for any amplifier containing a feedback loop to be completely stable. The gain of such an amplifier, as measured from the input back to the point where the feedback circuit connects to the input, must be less than unity at the frequency where the feedback voltage is in phase with the input voltage of the amplifier. If the gain is equal to or greater than unity at the frequency where the feedback voltage is in phase with the input, the amplifier will oscillate. This fact imposes a limitation on the amount of feedback, which may be employed in an amplifier that is to remain stable.

Early single-ended amplifiers did not have feedback loops; the cathode resistor in each stage could provide local feedback. An unbypassed resistance provides the greatest degree of linearization in a common cathode amplifier. All of the feedback occurs in a cathode follower; this is not useful if any kind of gain is required. The use of feedback has a few side effects. Feedback inherently tries to eliminate distortion so that the output is a larger version of the input. When feedback was introduced into triode amplifier circuits, the even harmonic distortion was diminished. The sound of a pentode amplifier improves with feedback, and has constant gain up to its full output limit. Decoupling the feedback loop at a high frequency gives the amplifier a more present sound. Hence, the creation of the *presence control*—this enhances the higher frequencies, which are lost in most guitar speakers. Also available is a low-end boost or resonance control. One of the side effects of using a resonance circuit is that it affects the damping factor of the amplifier, making the bottom end response seem looser. This is why I add in a switchable feedback resistor to compensate for the loss across R3. You can change R1 and R2 to make the amp as tight or as loose as you like.

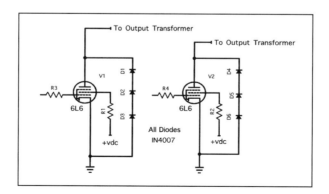

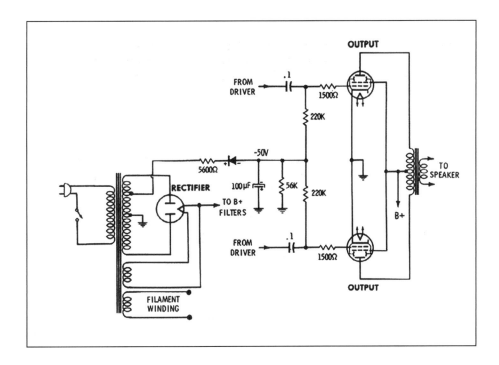

Output Tube Biasing

There are two basic methods of setting the bias current for output tubes, regardless of the class of operation. These methods are called *fixed bias* and *cathode bias*. Fixed biasing eliminates the cathode resistor and ties the cathode to ground. To obtain the same cathode current as a cathode bias circuit, you must apply a negative voltage to the grid. The signal adds and subtracts from the grid to turn the tube on and off. You can select any class of operation by making the bias voltage larger or smaller in magnitude, but the bias voltage must be negative. Because there isn't any limiting in the fixed bias circuit, output tube failure can be fatal to the components, whereas cathode biasing a circuit limits the current flow. Cathode biasing is one of the original forms of biasing and is the most common on single-ended power amps. The quiescent current is used to create a voltage drop across the cathode resistor. The grid is tied to ground through a resistor, and since the cathode is at a positive voltage, the grid looks negative with regard to the cathode, and the tube is self-biased by the cathode resistor. The bias control is like the fuel adjustment in an older car's carburetor—that is to say, there is an optimum setting point for your amplifier.

When an amp is *over-biased*, it is idling too low, so the tubes are running cold. This will cause your amplifier to sound dirty or more distorted, and to have a lower power output. The amp will seem lifeless and have too much crossover distortion.

When an amp is *under-biased*, it is idling too high, so the tubes are running very hot. The amplifier will seem to have more power. The plates will glow bright red from internal heat, which will cause them to burn out faster and short out, possibly destroying the output transformer.

Fixed Bias/Cathode Bias Switching

Vintage guitar amplifiers produce tones that are more mellow and "round" than the newer amps of today—this is the reason for the resurgence of amp companies that are building amplifiers with older styles of circuitry. Some players like the sound of cathode bias because they feel it has a better distortion sound, whereas fixed bias, which is more efficient, sounds harsher. With the addition of a bypass cap on the cathode, it produces more of the sweet, darker tone that is preferred; taking the cap out enhances the high-end response. This could also be a selectable feature by adding a separate switch to bring the capacitor (C1) in and out. R2 should be a wirewound resistor, 10 to 20 watts: 500 ohms for a pair of EL-34s or 6L6s, and 800 ohms for a pair of 6v6s. If an electrolytic is used at C1, make sure that you tie the negative to ground.

Bias Circuit 1

This circuit is designed around a Fender amp biasing design. Of course, you can use it for any amplifier that you wish.

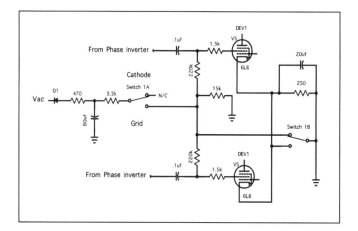

Bias Circuit 2

This circuit is designed around a Marshall biasing design.

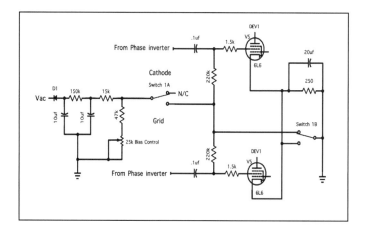

Biasing Your Amplifier with a Fixed Bias

Standard Biasing

6550A	-48v to -58v
EL-34	-38v to —48v
6CA7 6L6GC	-40v to -48v
6V6	-26v to —35v

This is the way most companies and repair shops would bias your amplifier. You need a multimeter to adjust the negative bias voltage. Before you turn your amplifier on, take out your output tubes. Next, attach the negative lead from your multimeter to the ground or chassis of your amp. Then, turn on the amp and put the positive lead of your multimeter to pin 5 on 6V6, 6L6, EL-34, 6CA7, 6550, KT-88, or pin 2 on EL-84. Adjust to the suggested voltage: Go by either by the specifications of the amplifier or tube manufacturer. Turn the amp off, reinstall the output tubes, make sure that a speaker is plugged in *(this is very important!)*, and then turn the amp back on. Let the amp warm up and stabilize for a couple of minutes, and then recheck the bias again and adjust if needed. The bias will change over time and use. This type of biasing is good for getting your amp in the ballpark before you try to shunt bias your amp (below).

Transformer Shunt Method

6550A	40 to 75 ma
EL-34	35 to 45 ma
6CA7 6L6GC	30 to 35 ma
6V6	22 to 27 ma
EL-84	22 to 27 ma

This method is accurate and fast. The tube bias alters how much current the tube will pass. Since all of the current leaves the output tube directly into the output transformer, you can shunt the output transformer with an ampmeter and measure the current directly. The negative lead from the ampmeter should go to the plate of the output tube, and the positive lead should go to the center tap of the output transformer, or the finish winding on a single-ended power amp's transformer. Adjust the amplifier to the desired current. If the amp has two output tubes or is a single-ended amp, set the bias to the single-tube bias rating. If the amplifier has four output tubes, then the reading on the meter must be divided in half. This method will work with just about any amplifier except the Fender 5E series.

Biasing Your Amplifier with a Cathode Bias

This type of biasing is time consuming and may take several different resistor values. First, hook up your ampmeter in the same way as for the shunt method. If the plate current is too low, a smaller value cathode resistor is needed; if the plate current is too high, a larger value cathode resistor is needed. Make sure you use the same or higher wattage cathode resistor.

Marshall Bias Mod 1 (6550 to EL-34)

The bias needs to be decreased by 10 V. This takes the replacement of two resistors on the 50- and 100-watt amps. The first thing you need to do is to locate the bias circuit of the amplifier; it should be located toward the right end of the circuitboard if the amp chassis is flipped over with the control pots facing you. Also, you should look up the schematic to see the values that need changing. For the 50-watt versions, change the 150-K resistor that comes from the power transformer to a 220-K. Change the 47-K resistor that is tied to one side of the bias pot with a 56-K resistor. On the 100-watt versions, you need to change the 15-K resistor that comes from the power transformer to a 27-K. After you replace these resistors, take out the output tubes and plug in the amplifier and turn it on. Take your multimeter and check your bias by connecting the negative lead of your multimeter to the ground or chassis of the amp and connect the positive lead to pin 5 of the output tube. Adjust the bias to -40 to -42 V. If you can't get the bias to go this low, increase the value of the resistor that is connected to the power transformer. Reinstall the output tubes. ***Make sure that you have a speaker load,*** and turn on the amplifier. You now need to set the bias voltage correctly.

Marshall Bias Mod 2 (EL-34 to 6550)

This is the same as the above, except that you should reverse the resistor values. On the 50-watter, change the 220-K to a 150-K resistor, and change the 56-K to a 47-K resistor. On the 100-watter change the 27-K to a 15-K resistor. Set the bias for −50 V. Reinstall the tubes and then correctly bias the amp.

Fender Silver to Blackface Bias Mod

This changes the bias/balance to a straight bias control, which allows better bias adjust to the output tubes.

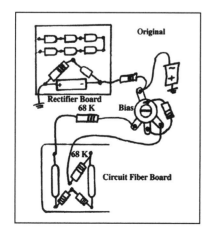
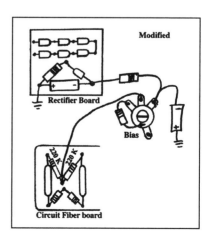

Master Volume Controls

The master volume control can be placed in various positions of the amplifier gain stages; it allows the preamp gain stages to distort while the power amp runs clean. It also allows you to create your tone at any playing volume.

Master 1

This is a standard master volume control that you can add to just about every amplifier on the market. Find the tone circuit (treble control center lead) or the last circuit before the phase inverter and insert the control pot. You can add a 47-K resistor in line from the treble control to prevent loading down the previous stage.

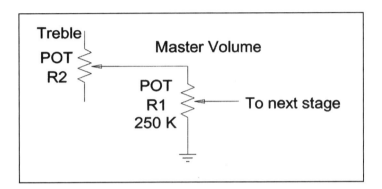

Master 2 (Output Attenuator)

This master allows you to drive all of the preamp stages—including the phase inverter—before the power amp. This master sounds more like a power attenuator or a soak. It gives you the best, distorted sound at any volume and, like Master 1, all you have to install is a control. As the control brings each out-of-phase signal closer to zero, cancellation occurs.

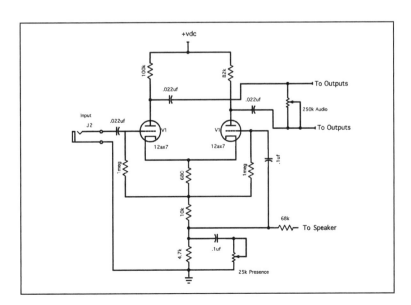

Master 3

This is a master volume with a distortion generator circuit. If you don't want to add another control for the distortion, tie the D1 and D2 to ground.

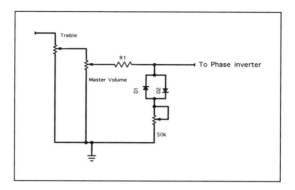

Distortion Generator 1

These circuits can be used in multiple positions, both before and after gain stages. These circuits can also be used on solidstate gain circuits. You can use a variety of diodes: IN914, IN4148, LEDs. They all sound different, and even have different colored LEDs.

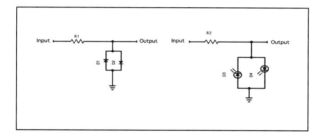

Distortion Generator 2

This is a cool circuit for adding distortion before the tone controls, so you can shape the distortion sound before the next stage.

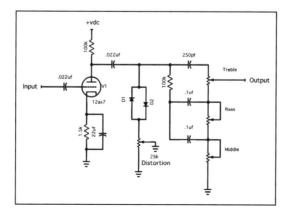

I have been asked over and over again what I did to George Lynch's, Steve Vai's, and Zakk Wylde's amplifiers. The best way to answer this question is to say that they all have combinations of the circuits that I'm showing you in this book. Most players want extra gain for better distortion, effects loops to put their rack effects in, and some type of switching so that they can switch back and fourth from the multiple sounds they want to use.

With tube amplifiers, there is no limit to the tonal possibilities that you can create. Because of the internal structure of an amplifier, modification is easily accomplished. Have fun and experiment—but be sure that you experiment on your own amp instead of a client's, as this will save you a lot of headaches. And if you're modifying one of your own amps, make sure that you don't start hours before your next concert!

Fender Concert Phase Inverter Mod

This amplifier was a great idea. The only problem was that Fender made the output stage too tight, making the distortion sound bad. Also, the 12AT7 needed to be changed to a 12AX7 to warm up the sound. Change the components to the values in parentheses. You can use any type of components—I personally like metal film resistors and polys for the capacitors. Also, it's a good idea to add the mid-boost circuit to this mod.

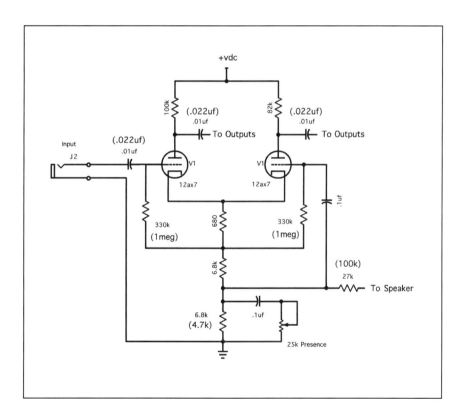

Marshall Mod

This mod can be done on any early two- and four-input Marshalls. It also works great on JCM 800 series amps. As I said earlier, it doesn't take a lot to make a tube amp sound amazing. This modification enhances the gain and distortion, and makes the amp have great distortion at low volumes. This was one of the most popular add-on mods for Steve Vai and George Lynch. It's a good idea to add the mid-boost circuit to this mod.

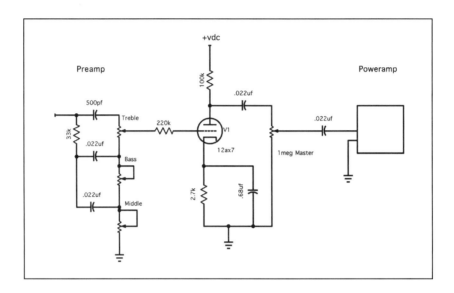

Six-Position Mid-Boost Mod

This control adds boost to the mid frequency and overall gain of your instrument, and can be used in any tube amp. This switch can make a fat guitar sound thinner, and a thin guitar sound fatter. The switch part of the circuit can be added to Marshall and Fender tone circuits.

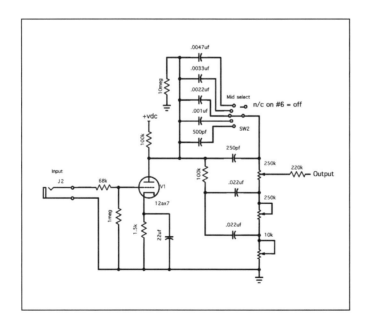

Marshall Super Bass to Super Lead Mod

This modification will work with four-input 200-, 100-, and 50-watt amps. Locate the first preamp tube (the one that is the farthest from the power transformer), and find its pin 3 (it's connected to an 820-ohm resistor with a 250-uF capacitor). From pin 3 there is a jumper wire across the tube socket—remove this wire, but leave the 820-ohm resistor and 250-uF capacitor connected to pin 3. From pin 8, run a wire to a 2.7-K resistor to ground. Tie a .68-uF capacitor across the 2.7-K that is going to pin 8. Now, locate pin 6 (it connects to a 100-K resistor). There is a .022-uF capacitor; remove this and replace it with a .0022-uF capacitor. Locate the treble pot. From the right side of the treble pot, a wire goes to the circuitboard and connects to a 250-pF capacitor; replace the 250-pF with a 500-pF capacitor. The opposite end of the 500-pF capacitor connects to a 56-K resistor; change this 56-K resistor to a 33-K. Locate the volume control of the first channel—across the center and the right-hand terminal—and install a .005-uF capacitor. Locate the third tube (phase inverter), and then locate pin 1 and pin 6, which each run to an individual .1-uF capacitor; replace the .1-uF capacitors with .022-uF capacitors. You can add gain to this mod by locating the second tube socket pin 3. Follow the wire to the circuitboard (it should be tied to an 820-ohm or 1-K resistor), and tie a .68-uF capacitor across the resistor. This will add gain and high end.

Tube Mods

As older tubes become harder and harder to find, you will need to modify the old tube sockets to accept newer style tubes. Here are several modifications that can help you with your older equipment.

Tube Mod 1 (83 Rectifier)

This tube was used on old Fenders, one of which is the Bassman 410. You can mod the socket to accept 5AR4, 5U4, 5V4, 5Y3, and rectifier tubes. Rewire the socket as follows.

1. Move the red wire on pin 2 to pin 4.

2. Move the yellow wire on pin 1 to pin 2.

3. Move both the yellow wire and the cloth wire on pin 4 to pin 8.

4. Move the red wire on pin 3 to pin 6. You should have a red wire on pin 4, a red wire on pin 6, a yellow wire on pin 2, a yellow wire on pin 8, and a wire going from pin 8 to the stand-by switch.

Tube Mod 2 (6SC7 to 12AX7)

This mod is a little more extensive. You will need to replace the socket with a 9-pin, and you will need to figure out a way to plug the larger hole of the 6SC7 socket.

1. Move pin 2 (6SC7) to pin 1 (12AX7).

2. Move pin 3 (6SC7) to pin 2 (12AX7).

3. Move pin 6 (6SC7) to pins 3 and 8 (12AX7).

4. Move pin 7 (6SC7) to pins 4 and 5 (12AX7).

5. Move pin 5 (6SC7) to pin 6 (12AX7).

6. Move pin 4 (6SC7) to pin 7 (12AX7).

7. Move pin 8 (6SC7) to pin 9 (12AX7).

Tube Mod 3 (7199 to 6AN8)

1. Leave the wires on pins 1, 4, and 5.

2. Move the original pin 2 to the new pin 6.

3. Move the original pin 3 to the new pin 7.

4. Move the original pin 6 to the new pin 9.

5. Move the original pin 7 to the new pin 8.

6. Move the original pin 8 to the new pin 3.

7. Move the original pin 9 to the new pin 2, and you're ready to go.

Power Supplies

Vacuum tubes and solidstate devices require an essentially pure DC power supply for proper operation. Primary power is usually taken from the home electrical supply. For DC voltages you need a transformer, a rectifier, and a filter (capacitors) to supply higher and lower DC voltages for the proper operation of various circuits in the equipment. This sort of sys-

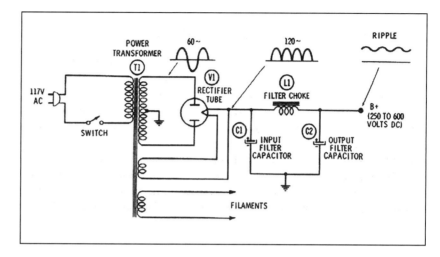

tem is designed so that it is capable of delivering the required current at a specific voltage. There is then a degree of regulation consistent with the requirements of the product, so its ripple level at full current is low for the load which will be fed, and none of the components will be overloaded with the type of operation considered. The design for the power supply for use in a particular application may best be accomplished through a series of steps.

The first step is to establish the operating requirements.

1. Output voltage required under full load.

2. Minimum, normal, and peak output current.

3. Voltage regulation required over the current range.

4. Ripple voltage limit.

5. Rectifier circuit used.

The output voltage required of the power supply is established by the operating conditions of the tubes that it will supply. The current rating of the supply is not necessarily tied down by a particular tube combination. It is always best to design a power supply in such a manner that it will have the greatest degree of flexibility. The minimum current drain taken from a power supply will be, in most cases, the bleeder current. The normal current rating of a power supply is usually a round number value chosen on the basis of the transformers and chokes. The current rating of a supply to feed a steady load should be at least equal to the steady drain of the load. Since the current drain of a power supply can vary over a large magnitude, it is important to determine what happens to the output voltage of the supply with regard to change in current. *Power supply regulation* may be expressed in terms of static and dynamic regulation. *Static regulation* relates to the regulation under long-term conditions of change in load, whereas dynamic regulation relates to short-term changes in load conditions.

Regulation is expressed as a change in output voltage with respect to load. The alternating component of the output voltage of a DC supply is the *ripple voltage;* it is superimposed on the DC voltage, and the effectiveness of the filter system can be expressed in terms of the ratio of the RMS (root-mean-square) value of the ripple voltage to the DC output voltage of the supply. Good design practice calls

for a ripple voltage of less than five percent of the supply voltage. Ripple frequency is related to the number of pulsations per second in the output of the filter system. A full-wave rectifier, having two pulses of 60 Hz, produces a 120 Hz ripple wave. There are two types of filter capacitors: *paper dielectric* and *electrolytic.* Paper capacitors consist of two strips of metal foil separated by several layers of special paper; in some capacitors, some of the paper is wax-impregnated, and in others it is oil-impregnated and oil-filled. Electrolytic capacitors consist of two aluminum electrodes in contact with a conducting film that acts as an electrolyte. A very thin film of oxide is formed on the surface of one electrode (anode); the film of oxide acts as the dielectric. Electrolytic capacitors can be greatly reduced in size by the use of etched aluminum foil for the anode. This increases the surface area and the dielectric film covering it.

Decoupled Supplies

When using multiple tube gain stages, you will need to decouple the power supply between the stages. If you don't do this, the chance for cross-talk between the stages is high. This is especially true when you are designing a multi-channel amplifier and don't want the signal of one channel to bleed into the next. The amount of filtering that you use in your gain stages is critical: Too low and the isolation is poor, too high and you suck the life out of the gain stage. You will need to decouple most of the modifications that I show in this book, especially if you are adding an effects loop or reverb circuit. Don't be afraid to experiment.

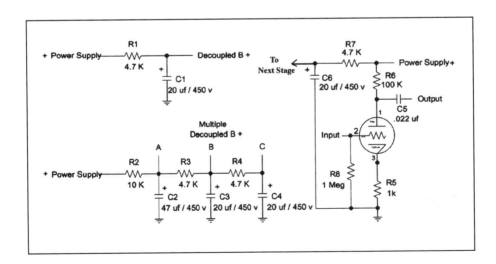

Rectifier Mod 1

Older amplifiers that used a tube rectifier are some of the most sought after. The natural sagging of the power supply causes the amplifier to have a smoother or warmer sound. With this modification, you can add some of that sag to a solidstate rectifier power supply. And, if you like, you can

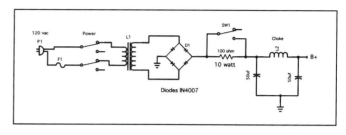

add a switch to the circuit so that you can switch between a hard (no sag) or soft (sag) sound. You can also put the resistor only on the output transformers B+ supply. This will cause the output tubes to sag but not the preamp section; this mod will lower the output power a little.

Rectifier Mod 2

There are multiple uses for this circuit. One option is that it can replace the tube rectifier if you are tired of your sound or can't find a replacement. Another option is if you want more output out of your amplifier with the higher plate voltages, or if you want the ability to switch between the two different sounds: hard (diodes) and soft (tube rectifier). One word of caution—when you add the diodes, this raises the supply voltage about 25 percent to around 500 VDC, and this may be higher than the rated voltages on the filter capacitors, which are generally 450 VDC. So, you might have to replace them with higher-voltage capacitors. This circuit works with all tube rectifiers: 5AR4, 5U4, 5V4, and 5Y3

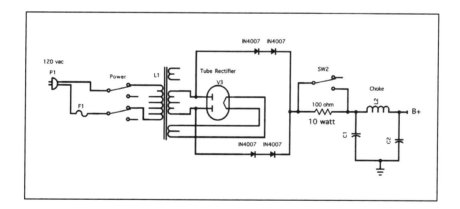

WARNING!

On both of these modifications, if you are going to use the switch function, I suggest that you use a large-frame DPDT rated at least 240 VAC. Also, don't mount the switch to the front panel of the amplifier. This is high voltage, and it can kill you.

Transient Response Mod

This modification can be done to any tube amp. It will improve the transient response of the power supply to the preamp tubes. You need to add a 1N4007 diode in series with the B+ line coming off the second filter supply capacitor; it should be after the choke if it has one. This will come before the supply capacitors feeding the phase inverter and preamp section. The cathode (bar) of the diode should face the next preamp stage, and the anode should be connected to the second filter supply capacitor/choke. When the output tubes pull current from the supply, the supply sags. The diode turns off during this sag and isolates the splitter and preamp stages.

Standby Switches

Why does your amp have a standby switch? The standby switch turns off or on the high voltage to the tubes, and the tubes will not draw any current without the high voltage to attract the negative electrons being emitted from the hot cathode. They will still draw heater current, but with the standby "off," output tube life is extended. When you first turn your amplifier "on," it is very important that you leave your standby "off" for at least a minute. This allows the heaters to get the cathode to the correct temperature so it can emit its electrons. After the cathode is emitting its electrons, the high voltage can be applied. If the high voltage is applied before the cathode is ready, it will cause *cathode stripping*—the high voltage on the plate will rip the electrons from the cathode material. Most high-powered amplifiers have an HT or B+ fuse, which is in line with the standby switch. "HT" stands for "high tension" in Great Britain, by the way.

Marshall 50-Watt Bias Mod

Early '70s Marshalls came from the factory with the bias circuit connected to the cold side of the standby switch. The cold side of the switch is the side that doesn't have the B+ (high) voltage on it when the switch is "off." This causes the output tubes to get both the bias and the plate (high) voltage at the same time. This is bad and will cause cathode stripping, which shortens the life of your tubes. To check to see if you have one of these amps, pull out your output tubes, and turn your amp on, leaving the standby "off." With your voltmeter, put the negative lead on the amplifier chassis (ground), and the positive lead to pin 5 of one of the output tube sockets. If you read a voltage, then you will not need to change your amp. If not, then determine what terminals on the switch are cold. Find the wire coming from the bias diode. Generally, it will be the only terminal on the switch with two wires on it. Move this wire to the other side of the switch. Now, test the amp again like you did earlier with the output tubes out and see if you have a bias voltage. If not, you moved the wire to the wrong terminal on the standby switch.

WARNING!

You must unplug your amplifier and discharge the power supply capacitors before you do this modification. The amplifier has very high voltages that hurt and can kill!

HT Fuse (B+)

Put a fuse in the B+ (power supply) line after the rectifier tube or silicon diodes and before the first filter capacitors. This can save your power and output transformer if you get a shorted filter capacitor or output tube. It could even save an output tube socket if the fuse blows fast enough. Even if you don't have the room to install a panel-mount fuse holder, you can get an internal chassis-mount fuse holder, which doesn't take up any room at all.

Heaters

The heater-type cathode was developed as a result of the requirement for a type of emitter that could be operated from alternating current and yet would not introduce AC ripple modulation even when used in low-level stages. It essentially consists of a small nickel-alloy cylinder with a coating of strontium and barium oxides on its surface similar to the oxide-coated filament. Inside the cylinder is an insulated heater element consisting (usually) of a double spiral of tungsten wire. The heater may operate on any voltage from 2- to 117-V AC or DC, although 6.3 V is the most popular. The heater operates at quite a high temperature so that the cathode itself is brought to operating temperature in a matter of 15 to 30 seconds. Heat coupling between the heater and the cathode is mainly by radiation, although there is some thermal conduction through the insulating coating on the heater wire, since this coating is also in contact with the cathode thimble.

DC Heaters 1

AC heaters are not the best way to go. There is some hum induced into the signal path by virtue of having AC voltages inside the tube. The only way to eliminate this is to operate the heater from direct current. We need to generate either 6 or 12 VDC for proper cathode operation. If you were to rectify the 6.3-VAC heaters, you would get 9 VDC, which is too high for the 6.3-V heaters. The only option is to regulate the DC to 6.3 VDC. Here are several circuits for obtaining the regulated heaters. This circuit requires a second transformer to get the supply current needed.

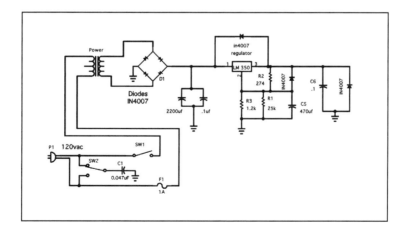

DC Heaters 2

This regulator can be used with an existing heater supply.

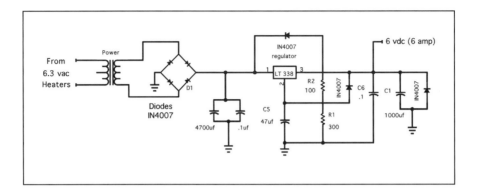

Soft Start for Power Tubes

Why Tubes Fail

In tubes, the dominant cause for failure is a filament breakdown in cold start. Repeated heating and cooling, plus the stress of the initial cold-current surge, cause slow deterioration of the filament. You can see a bright initial light flash in the filaments of some tubes at startup, especially when they are operated with AC heaters. This shows clearly how large the initial current surge is. For maximum life, tubes should be on for long periods of time, and the cold-current surge should be eliminated.

In power tubes, the filament must deliver such a high electron flow that the filament also wears away, as in an incandescent lamp. The cold-current surge then eventually breaks the filament. Deformation of the electrode structures due to overloading can cause premature failure in power tubes. Optimal use requires minimizing the active time with heavy anode current and eliminating the cold-current surge. In all tubes, the full plate voltage should not be applied until the filaments are warmed up to prevent cathode stripping. Cold-current surge is a serious problem in power amp sections. The resistance of a cold 6L6 filament is three to four times higher than when it is hot. A 6L6 that draws 0.9 amps hot draws 3 amps cold.

Soft Start 1

This circuit runs off your 6.3 VDC heaters. If you don't have DC heaters you can add a small separate transformer to power it. You need a 5-VDC relay to turn your B+ supply on and off. The contacts on the relay have to accept at least 240 VAC. These circuits are great if your amplifier does not have a standby switch.

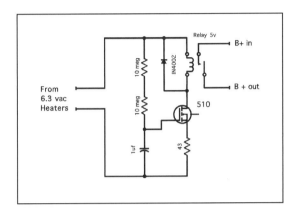

Soft Start 2

This circuit will work right off your standard AC heaters.

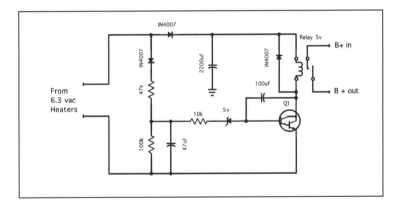

Switching Circuits

The switching method is determined by the end-user's operational requirements. Many devices can be used as switch elements in an amplifier. The most important distinction is whether the switch is electronic or mechanical. Electronic devices include bipolar junction transistors, JFETs, MOSFETs, and LDRs (more about those in a moment). Mechanical switches include both ones that are manually operated and relays. The ideal switch is one where the resistance between the contacts is infinite when the switch is open or off-state, and there is zero contact resistance when the switch is closed or on-state. In the next set of circuits, I am going to show you various ways to turn on or off and switch in or out various features on your amplifiers.

Switch 1

Here is a circuit for switching a single light-detecting resistor (LDR) in a circuit with an LED indicator. This circuit is set up to power an LED on an external footswitch.

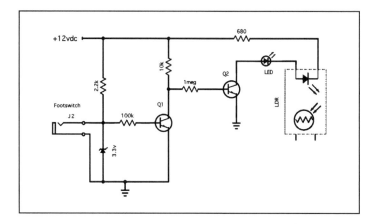

Switch 2

This is also an LDR switching circuit. This should be used when you want two states, but it can also be used for channel switching an amplifier or switching an effects loop in or out. This circuit is setup to power an external footswitch LED.

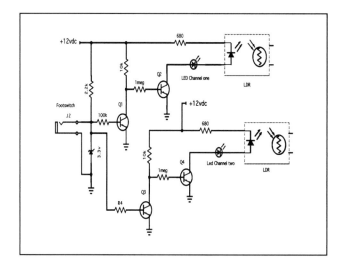

On the following three circuits, I like to use 2N5210s and MPS A13s for the transistors, and VTL5C7s for the LDRs.

Switch 3

This circuit is used for switching preamp or master volume controls; it uses the Switch 2 circuit to power the LDRs.

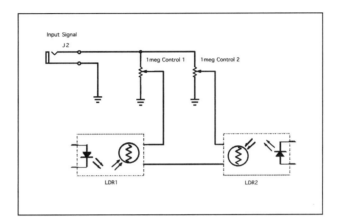

Switch 4

Here is a combination of switching possibilities with LDRs. In all of these circuits you can use Switch 2 to power the LDRs.

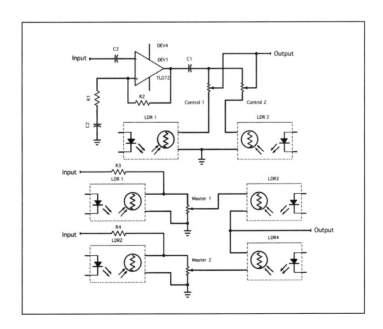

Switch 5

I designed this switching circuit to switch in and out effects loops 1 and 2. The lower diagram shows how to place the LDRs in the amplifier circuit between the preamp and the power amp stages. This circuit is designed to power an external footswitch LED.

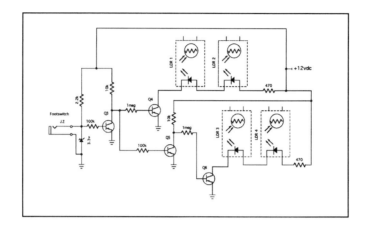

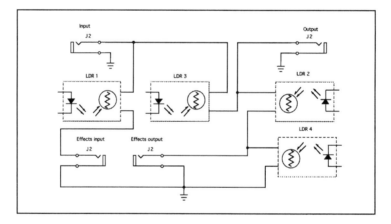

Footswitch Circuit

Here are two circuits for a footswitch pedal: one with and one without an LED indicator.

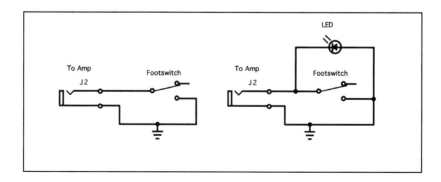

Switch 6

This is a switching circuit for a relay. You can make the relay between 5 and 12 VDC. It depends on the "+" voltage that you put on the positive side of the relay. Q9 basically supplies the ground to the relay. This circuit can be used to switch an effects loop in and out, or to turn a preamp function on and off. This circuit is designed to power an external footswitch LED.

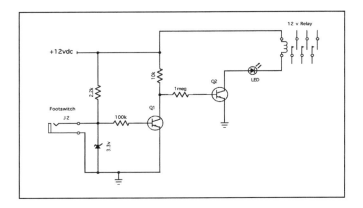

Switch 7

This is a great circuit for channel-switching multiple channels on an amplifier, or anywhere you need two states. This circuit also powers an external footswitch LED.

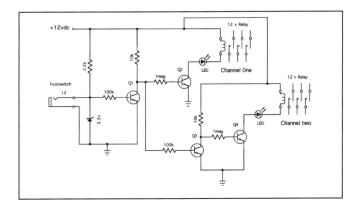

Switch 8

This can be used to switch preamp or master volume controls; use Switch 6.

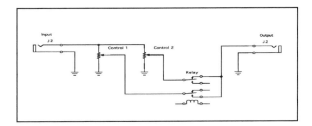

Switch 9

This is a field-effect transistor (FET) switching driver circuit with LED indicators. This circuit can be used to drive the FET circuits on Switch 10. It is designed to power an external footswitch LED; you can also use this circuit to mix FETs and LDRs by putting the LDRs in series with the LEDs.

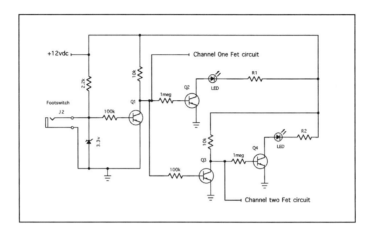

Switch 10

Here is a combination of switching possibilities with FETs. In these circuits, you can use Switch 9 to power the FETs. I use J112 FETs for these circuits. I would use these circuits for lower power applications like solidstate preamps where you are not going to put high-level signals through them. This is why I put the FETs on the ground leg of the control pots after the tube gain stage. These also work great for reverb return switching.

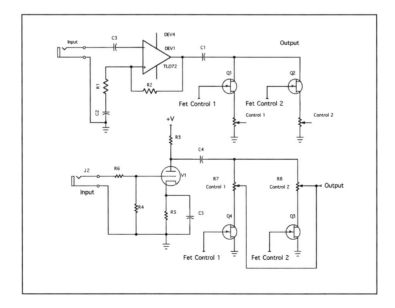

Fender Channel Footswitch Mod

This circuit allows you to tie two Fender Concert, Deluxe Rev II, or Twin Rev II amplifiers, and allows you to switch their functions in unison with one footswitch. The best way to do this modification is to cannibalize one of the two footswitches that come with the amplifiers, since Fender uses a custom cable in their footswitches.

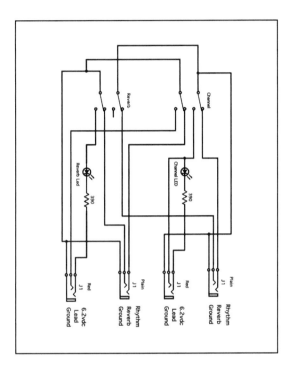

Fender Vibrato "Ticking" Cure

The ticking caused by the vibrato is caused by improper lead dress. It can be cured by connecting an .01-uF, 600-V Mylar capacitor on the 10-meg resistor in the vibrator circuit. Also, make sure that you dress the leads to the vibrato speed and intensity controls away from the tone controls and filter leads. Bunch the leads to the components on the fiber circuitboard parts panel, which connects to the tube socket of the 12AX7a vibrato tube.

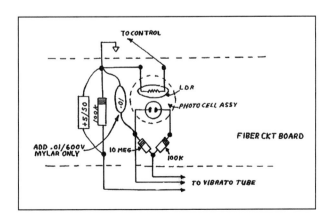

CHAPTER 7
TUBE SPECIFICATIONS

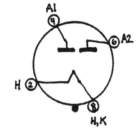

HIGH VACUUM   **5AR4**

FULL-WAVE RECTIFIER   **GZ34**

Glass octal-type used as a full-wave rectifier capable of I_{OUT} (DC) = 250mA. Indirectly heated cathode is direct-connected to the heater, which has a controlled turn-on delay.

Physical:

Maximum overall length	87mm
Maximum seated height	71mm
Diameter	38mm

Heater Requirements:

5V AC or DC
1,900 mA

Maximum Ratings
(per section):

PIV	1,500	V
V_A (RMS)	550	V
V_F (I_K=125mA)	60	V
I_A (pk)	750	mA
I_K (DC)	250	mA

Maximum Circuit Values:

$C_K \leq 60\mu F$ for first capacitor of LC pi-filter or main input of capacitive filter

Full-wave rectifier - Capacitor input filter, $C \leq 60\mu F$

V_A (RMS)	300	350	400	450	500	550	V
I_K (DC)	250	250	250	250	200	160	mA
V_K (DC)	330	380	430	480	560	640	V
R_{LIMIT} (per plate)	75	100	125	150	175	200	Ω

Full-wave rectifier - Choke filter, L = 10H, C = 4μF to 60μF, R_{LIMIT} = 0Ω

V_A (RMS)	300	350	400	450	500	550	V
I_K (DC)	250	250	250	250	250	225	mA
V_K (DC)	250	290	330	375	420	465	V

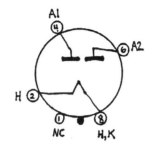

A1
④
⑥ A2
H ②
①
⑧
NC
H,K

HIGH-VACUUM   5U4GB
FULL-WAVE RECTIFIER   GZ32

Glass octal-type used as full-wave rectifier in medium- and high-power equipment. May be mounted in any position provided adequate ventilation is present, and pins 1 and 4 are vertically aligned for horizontal mounting.

Physical:

Maximum overall length	118mm
Maximum seated height	104mm
Diameter	40mm

Heater Requirements: 5V AC or DC
3,000 mA

Maximum Ratings
(per section):

PIV	1,550	V
V_A (RMS)	550	V
V_F (I_K=275mA)	50	V
I_A (pk)	4,600	mA
I_K (DC)	1,000	mA

Maximum Circuit Values: $C_K \leq 80\mu F$ for first capacitor of LC pi-filter or main input of capacitive filter

Full-v Full-wave rectifier:

	Capacitor Input Filter		Choke Input Filter L = 10H, C = 60μF	
V_A (RMS)	300	450	550	V
I_K (DC)	300	275	275	mA
V_K (DC)	290	460	420	V
R_{LIMIT}	21	67	----	Ω
C_K	40	40	—	μF

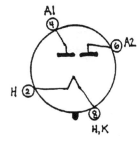

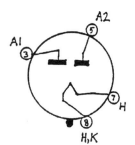

FULL-WAVE	**5Y3GT**
RECTIFIER	**5Y4GT**

Glass octal-type used as full-wave rectifier in low-power equipment. May be mounted in any position provided adequate ventilation is present, and:

1) For 5Y3GT - pins 2 and 3 are vertically aligned for horizontal mounting.

2) For 5Y4GT - pins 1 and 4 are vertically aligned for horizontal mounting.

Physical:

Maximum overall length	86mm	
Maximum seated height	72mm	
Diameter	33mm	

Heater Requirements:

5V AC or DC
2,000 mA

Maximum Ratings (per section):

PIV	1,400	V
V_A (RMS)	500	V
V_F (I_K=125mA)	60	V
I_A (pk)	2,200	mA
I_K (DC)	400	mA

Maximum Circuit Values:

$C_K \leq 60\mu F$ for first capacitor of LC pi-filter or main input of capacitive filter

	Capacitor Input Filter	Choke Input Filter L = 10H, C = 10µF	
V_A (RMS)	350	500	V
I_K (DC)	125	125	mA
V_K (DC)	350	390	V
R_{LIMIT}	50	—	Ω
C_K	10	—	µF

6BQ5/EL84

Class A - Triode Operation

(Screen grid connected to plate)

Plate Voltage	250 volts
Common Cathode Resistance	270 Ω
Plate Load Resistance	3.5 KΩ
Plate Current (zero signal)	34 mA
Plate Current (max. signal)	36 mA
Input Signal Voltage (rms)	6.7 volts (rms
Power Output	1.95 watts
Percent Distortion	9.0 %

Class AB - Triode Operation

(Two tubes, push-pull. Screen grid connected to plate)

Plate Voltage	250	300 volts
Common Cathode Resistance	270	270 Ω
Plate to Plate Load Resistance	10	10 KΩ
Plate Current (zero signal)	2x20	2x24 mA
Plate Current (max. signal)	2x21.7	2x26.0 mA
Input Signal Voltage (rms)	8.3	10 volts (rms)
Power Output	3.4	5.2 watts
Percent Distortion	2.5	2.5 %

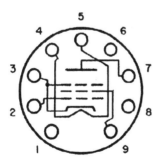

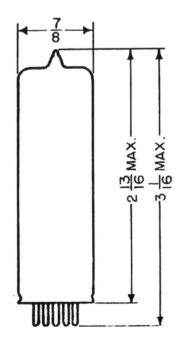

PIN CONNECTIONS

PIN.NO.	ELEMENT
1. —	INTERNALLY CONNECTED
2. —	GRID NO. 1.
3. —	CATHODE AND GRID NO. 3.
4. —	FILAMENT
5. —	FILAMENT
6. —	INTERNALLY CONNECTED
7. —	ANODE
8. —	INTERNALLY CONNECTED
9. —	GRID NO. 2.

6CA7/EL34

TENTATIVE DATA

Class AB₁ Audio Amplifier
Distributed Load Connection

←

Maximum Ratings (Design Center Values)

Plate and Grid No. 2 Supply Voltage	500 V
Plate Dissipation	25 W
Grid No. 2 Dissipation	8 W
Cathode Current	150 mA
Grid Current Starting Point - Grid No. 1 Voltage when	
Grid No. 1 Current is 0.3 μA	−1.3 V
Grid No. 1 Circuit Resistance	500 KΩ
External Resistance Between Heater and Cathode	20 KΩ
Voltage Between Heater and Cathode	100 V

Typical Operation (Fixed Bias - Two Tubes Push Pull)

Plate Supply Voltage	500 V
Grid No. 2 Supply Voltage	(See Note 1)
Grid No. 1 Bias	(approx.) −44.5 V
Plate to Plate Load Resistance	7000 Ω
Plate and Grid No. 2 Current (Zero Signal)	2x57 mA
Plate and Grid No. 2 Current (Max Signal)	2x112 mA
Input Signal Voltage (rms)	32 V
Power Output	60 W
Harmonic Distortion	2.5 %

Note 1:

Screen voltage is obtained from taps located at 43% of the plate winding turns.
An unbypassed resistor of 1 KΩ in series with each screen grid is necessary
to prevent screen overload.

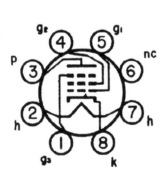

PIN CONNECTIONS

NO.1- GRID NO.3

NO.2- HEATER

NO.3- PLATE

NO.4- GRID NO.2

NO.5- GRID NO.1

NO.6- N.C.

NO.7- HEATER

NO.8- CATHODE

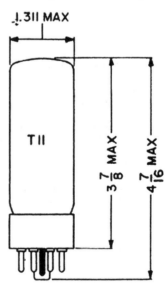

Revised 9/60

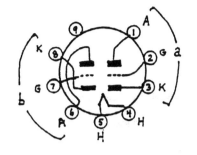

MEDIUM-MU   6CG7
TWIN TRIODE   6FQ7

A miniature 9-pin medium-mu dual triode used in RF and audio frequency voltage amplifiers.

Similar to the octal-type 6SN7GTB within performance limits.

Physical:	Maximum overall length	67mm
	Maximum seated height	61mm
	Diameter	22mm

Heater Requirements: 6.3V AC or DC
600 mA

Maximum Ratings
(per section):

V_A	330	V		
P_A	4	W	5.7W both sections
I_A	22	mA		
V_{H-K}	200	V		
μ	20			

Maximum Circuit Values: R_{G1} 1MΩ, for fixed-bias operation.
2M2Ω, for cathode-bias operation

Typical Operating Values: common-cathode, $C_K \geq 1\mu F$

V+(V)	R_A (kΩ)	R_L (kΩ)	R_K (Ω)	E_{OUT}	A_V
250	47	47	1k30	59	14
	47	100	1k58	73	15
	47	220	1k80	83	16
	100	100	2k50	68	16
	100	220	3k13	82	16
	100	470	3k90	96	16
	220	220	4k80	68	16
	220	470	6k50	85	16
	220	1M	7k80	96	16

6EU7

TWIN TRIODE

MINIATURE TYPE

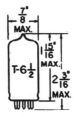

UNIPOTENTIAL CATHODE

HEATER

6.3±10% VOLTS   0.3 AMP.

AC OR DC

ANY MOUNTING POSITION

GLASS BULB

BOTTOM VIEW

SMALL-BUTTON NOVAL
9 PIN BASE
9LS

THE 6EU7 IS A HIGH-MU TWIN TRIODE IN THE 9 PIN MINIATURE CONSTRUCTION. IT IS ESPECIALLY DESIGNED FOR USE IN HIGH-GAIN RESISTANCE-COUPLED LOW-LEVEL AUDIO-AMPLIFIER APPLICATIONS, SUCH AS PREAMPLIFIERS FOR MONOPHONIC AND STEREOPHONIC PHONOGRAPHS, AND MICROPHONE AMPLIFIERS. THE BASING ARRANGE-MENT ENABLES THE CIRCUIT DESIGNER TO OBTAIN GOOD ISOLATION BETWEEN CHAN-ELS WHEN THE TUBE IS USED IN A STEREO SYSTEM.

DIRECT INTERELECTRODE CAPACITANCES
WITHOUT EXTERNAL SHIELD

	UNIT #1	UNIT #2	
GRID TO PLATE	1.5	1.5	μμf
GRID TO CATHODE AND HEATER	1.6	1.6	μμf
PLATE TO CATHODE AND HEATER	0.2	0.2	μμf

RATINGS
INTERPRETED ACCORDING TO DESIGN MAXIMUM SYSTEM

AMPLIFIER - CLASS A$_1$
VALUES ARE FOR EACH UNIT

HEATER VOLTAGE	6.3±10%	VOLTS
MAXIMUM PLATE VOLTAGE	330	VOLTS
MAXIMUM GRID VOLTAGE:		
NEGATIVE BIAS VALUE	55	VOLTS
POSITIVE BIAS VALUE	0	VOLTS
MAXIMUM PLATE DISSIPATION	1.2	WATTS
MAXIMUM PEAK HEATER-CATHODE VOLTAGE:		
HEATER NEGATIVE WITH RESPECT TO CATHODE	200[A]	VOLTS
HEATER POSITIVE WITH RESPECT TO CATHODE	200[A]	VOLTS

[A] THE DC COMPONENT MUST NOT EXCEED 100 VOLTS.

CONTINUED ON FOLLOWING PAGE

TUNG·SOL

6L6GB

BEAM PENTODE

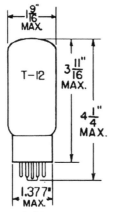

T-12

$1\frac{9}{16}"$ MAX.

$3\frac{11}{16}"$ MAX.

$4\frac{1}{4}"$ MAX.

1.377" MAX.

GLASS BULB

MEDIUM SHELL OR
SHORT MEDIUM SHELL
7 PIN OCTAL B7-12
OUTLINE DRAWING
JEDEC 12-15

COATED UNIPOTENTIAL CATHODE

HEATER
6.3±0.6 VOLTS   0.9 AMP.
AC OR DC

ANY MOUNTING POSITION

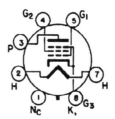

BOTTOM VIEW
BASING DIAGRAM
JEDEC 7S

THE 6L6GB IS A BEAM PENTODE DESIGNED WITH HIGH POWER SENSITIVITY AND HIGH EFFICIENCY FOR SERVICE IN THE OUTPUT STAGES OF AC RECEIVERS. IT IS CAPABLE OF DELIVERING AN OUTPUT AT ALL POWER LEVELS WITH A VERY LOW PERCENTAGE OF HARMONIC DISTORTION.

DIRECT INTERELECTRODE CAPACITANCES – APPROX.

GRID TO PLATE: G TO P	0.9	pf
INPUT: G_1 TO (H+K+G_2+BP)	11.5	pf
OUTPUT: P TO (H+K+G_2+BP)	9.5	pf

→ RATINGS

INTERPRETED ACCORDING TO DESIGN MAXIMUM SYSTEM

	TRIODE[A] CONNECTION	PENTODE CONNECTION	
HEATER VOLTAGE	6.3±0.6		VOLTS
MAXIMUM HEATER—CATHODE VOLTAGE:			
HEATER NEGATIVE WITH RESPECT TO CATHODE			
TOTAL DC AND PEAK	200		VOLTS
HEATER POSITIVE WITH RESPECT TO CATHODE			
TOTAL DC AND PEAK	200		VOLTS
DC	100		VOLTS
MAXIMUM PLATE VOLTAGE	300	400	VOLTS
MAXIMUM GRID #2 VOLTAGE	----	300	VOLTS
MAXIMUM PLATE DISSIPATION	22	22	WATTS
MAXIMUM GRID #2 DISSIPATION	----	2.8	WATTS
MAXIMUM GRID #1 CIRCUIT RESISTANCE:			
FIXED BIAS	0.1	0.1	MEGOHM
SELF BIAS	0.5	0.5	MEGOHM

[A] GRID #2 CONNECTED TO PLATE.

CONTINUED ON FOLLOWING PAGE

→ INDICATES A CHANGE.

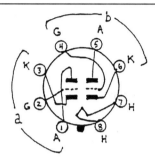

MEDIUM-MU
DUAL TRIODE

6SN7GTB

Glass octal type used as a resistance-coupled voltage amplifier or driver stage in audio frequency amplifiers. Also used as a horizontal-deflector oscillator in television sets.

May be mounted in any position if adequate ventilation is provided.

Physical:	Maximum overall length	84mm
	Maximum seated height	70mm
	Diameter	32mm

Heater Requirements: 6.3V AC or DC
                            600 mA

Maximum Ratings (per section):				
V_A	450	V		
P_A	5	W	7.5W both sections
I_A	20	mA	
V_{H-K}	200	V	
μ	20		

Maximum Circuit Values: R_{G1} 1MΩ, for fixed-bias operation
                               2M2Ω, for cathode-bias operation

 **ELECTRONICS**

6U10

COMPACTRON THREE-SECTION TRIODE

——————— DESCRIPTION AND RATING ———————

The 6U10 is a compactron containing two medium-mu triodes and one high-mu triode.

GENERAL

ELECTRICAL

Cathode - Coated Unipotential

Heater Characteristics and Ratings

	Series Circuit*	Parallel Circuit‡	
Heater Voltage, AC or DC . . .	6.3	6.3±0.6§	Volts
Heater Current	0.6±0.04§	0.6¶	Amperes
Heater Warm-up Time, Average# . .	11	---	Seconds

Direct Interelectrode CapacitancesΔ

	Section 1	Section 2	Section 3	
Grid to Plate: (g to p) .	1.3	1.3	1.2	pf
Input: g to (h + k), . .	1.7	1.5	1.8	pf
Output: p to (h + k) . .	0.26	0.28	0.9	pf

MECHANICAL

Operating Position - Any
Envelope - T-9, Glass
Base - E12-70, Button 12-Pin
Outline Drawing - EIA 9-56

Maximum Diameter. . .	1.188	Inches
Maximum Over-all Length	1.875	Inches
Maximum Seated Height .	1.500	Inches

MAXIMUM RATINGS

Design-Maximum ratings are limiting values of operating and environmental conditions applicable to a bogey electron tube of a specified type as defined by its published data and should not be exceeded under the worst probable conditions.

The tube manufacturer chooses these values to provide acceptable serviceability of the tube, making allowance for the effects of changes in operating conditions due to variations in the characteristics of the tube under consideration.

The equipment manufacturer should design so that initially and throughout life no design-maximum value for the intended service is exceeded with a bogey tube under the worst probable operating conditions with respect to supply-voltage variation, equipment component variation, equipment control adjustment, load variation, signal variation, environmental conditions, and variations in the characteristics of all other electron devices in the equipment.

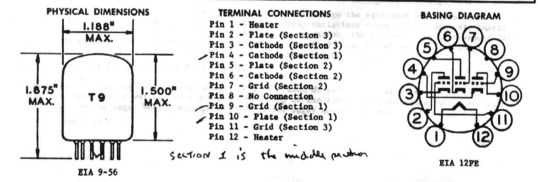

PHYSICAL DIMENSIONS

1.188" MAX.

1.875" MAX.   T 9   1.500" MAX.

EIA 9-56

TERMINAL CONNECTIONS

Pin 1 - Heater
Pin 2 - Plate (Section 3)
Pin 3 - Cathode (Section 3)
Pin 4 - Cathode (Section 1)
Pin 5 - Plate (Section 2)
Pin 6 - Cathode (Section 2)
Pin 7 - Grid (Section 2)
Pin 8 - No Connection
Pin 9 - Grid (Section 1)
Pin 10 - Plate (Section 1)
Pin 11 - Grid (Section 3)
Pin 12 - Heater

SECTION 1 is the middle section

BASING DIAGRAM

EIA 12FE

6U10 .

MAXIMUM RATINGS (Cont'd)

DESIGN-MAXIMUM VALUES	Sections 1 and 3	Section 2	
Plate Voltage.	330	330	Volts
Positive DC Grid Voltage	0	0	Volts
Negative DC Grid Voltage	50	50	Volts
Plate Dissipation	2.0	1.0	Watts
DC Cathode Current	20	---	Milliamperes
Heater-Cathode Voltage			
Heater Positive with Respect to Cathode			
DC Component	100	100	Volts
Total DC and Peak	200	200	Volts
Heater Negative with Respect to Cathode			
DC Component	100	100	Volts
Total DC and Peak	275	200	Volts
Grid Circuit Resistance**			
With Fixed Bias	1.0	0.5	Megohms
With Cathode Bias	2.0	1.0	Megohms

CHARACTERISTICS AND TYPICAL OPERATION

AVERAGE CHARACTERISTICS	Sections 1 and 3	Section 2	
Plate Voltage.	200	200	Volts
Grid Voltage	-6.0	-1.5	Volts
Amplification Factor	17.5	98	
Plate Resistance, approximate	7700	61000	Ohms
Transconductance.	2300	1600	Micromhos
Plate Current.	9.6	1.2	Milliamperes
Grid Voltage, approximate			
Ib = 100 Microamperes	-15	---	Volts
Grid Voltage, approximate			
Ib = 35 Microamperes	---	-3	Volts

NOTES

* Operated with the heater in series with the heaters of other tubes having the same bogey heater current.

‡ Operated with the heater in parallel with the heaters of other tubes having the same bogey heater voltage.

§ For parallel heater operation, the equipment designer should design the equipment so that heater voltage is centered at the specified bogey value, with heater supply variations restricted to maintain heater voltage within the specified tolerance; for series heater operation, the equipment designer should design the equipment so that heater current is centered at the specified bogey value, with heater supply variations restricted to maintain heater current within the specified tolerance.

¶ Heater current of a bogey tube at Ef = 6.3 volts.

♯ The time required for the voltage across the heater to reach 80 percent of the bogey value after applying 4 times the bogey heater voltage to a circuit consisting of the tube heater in series with a resistance equal to 3 times the bogey heater voltage divided by the bogey heater current.

Δ Without external shield.

** In applications where self-bias is used with Section 2, a maximum grid curcuit resistance of 10 megohms is permissible, provided that the plate supply voltage and load resistance are such that the plate dissipation can never exceed 0.5 watts.

BEAM PENTODE

6V6GTA

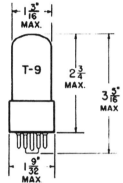

T-9

$1\frac{3}{16}$" MAX.

$2\frac{3}{4}$" MAX.

$3\frac{5}{16}$" MAX

$1\frac{9}{32}$" MAX

GLASS BULB

COATED UNIPOTENTIAL CATHODE

HEATER

6.3 VOLTS 0.45 AMP.

AC OR DC

ANY MOUNTING POSITION

BOTTOM VIEW

INTERMEDIATE SHELL
7 PIN OCTAL
7S

THE 6V6GTA IS A BEAM POWER AMPLIFIER DESIGNED FOR SERVICE IN THE OUTPUT STAGE OF 450 MA. SERIES HEATER OPERATED TV RECEIVERS. IT HAS HIGH POWER SENSITIVITY AND HIGH POWER OUTPUT WITH COMPARATIVELY LOW SUPPLY VOLTAGE. THERMAL CHARACTERISTICS OF THE HEATER ARE CONTROLLED SUCH THAT HEATER VOLTAGE SURGES DURING THE WARM-UP CYCLE ARE MINIMIZED PROVIDED IT IS USED WITH OTHER TYPES WHICH ARE SIMILARLY CONTROLLED. WITH THE EXCEPTION OF HEATER RATINGS, ITS CHARACTERISTICS ARE IDENTICAL TO THE 6V6GT.

DIRECT INTERELECTRODE CAPACITANCES

GRID TO PLATE: (G_1 TO P)	0.7	$\mu\mu f$
INPUT: G_1 TO ($H+K+G_2+G_3$)	9.0	$\mu\mu f$
OUTPUT: P TO ($H+K+G_2+G_3$)	7.5	$\mu\mu f$

RATINGS
INTERPRETED ACCORDING TO DESIGN CENTER VALUES

HEATER VOLTAGE	6.3	VOLTS
MAXIMUM HEATER—CATHODE VOLTAGE:		
HEATER POSITIVE WITH RESPECT TO CATHODE:		
DC	100	VOLTS
TOTAL DC AND PEAK	200	VOLTS
HEATER NEGATIVE WITH RESPECT TO CATHODE:		
TOTAL DC AND PEAK	200	VOLTS
MAXIMUM PLATE VOLTAGE	315	VOLTS
MAXIMUM GRID #2 VOLTAGE	285	VOLTS
MAXIMUM PLATE DISSIPATION	12	WATTS
MAXIMUM GRID #2 DISSIPATION	2	WATTS
MAXIMUM GRID #1 CIRCUIT RESISTANCE:		
FIXED BIAS OPERATION	0.1	MEGOHM
CATHODE BIAS OPERATION	0.5	MEGOHM

VERTICAL DEFLECTION AMPLIFIER — TRIODE CONNECTION[AB]

HEATER VOLTAGE	6.3	VOLTS
MAXIMUM DC PLATE VOLTAGE	315	VOLTS
MAXIMUM PEAK POSITIVE VOLTAGE (ABSOLUTE MAXIMUM)	1200	VOLTS
MAXIMUM PLATE DISSIPATION[C]	9	WATTS
MAXIMUM PEAK NEGATIVE GRID VOLTAGE	250	VOLTS
MAXIMUM AVERAGE CATHODE CURRENT	55	MA.
MAXIMUM PEAK CATHODE CURRENT	105	MA.
MAXIMUM GRID CIRCUIT RESISTANCE (CATHODE BIAS)	2.2	MEGOHMS
HEATER WARM-UP TIME (APPROX.)[*]	11.0	SECONDS

[A]ALL VALUES ARE EVALUATED ON DESIGN CENTER SYSTEM EXCEPT WHERE ABSOLUTE MAXIMUM IS STATED.

[B]FOR OPERATION IN A 525-LINE, 30-FRAME SYSTEM AS DESCRIBED IN "STANDARDS OF GOOD ENGINEERING PRACTICE FOR TELEVISION BROADCASTING STATIONS; FEDERAL COMMUNICATIONS COMMISSION". THE DUTY CYCLE OF THE VOLTAGE PULSE NOT TO EXCEED 15% OF A SCANNING CYCLE.

[C]IN STAGES OPERATING WITH GRID-LEAK BIAS, AN ADEQUATE CATHODE BIAS RESISTOR OR OTHER SUITABLE MEANS IS REQUIRED TO PROTECT THE TUBE IN THE ABSENCE OF EXCITATION.

[*]HEATER WARM-UP TIME IS DEFINED AS THE TIME REQUIRED FOR THE VOLTAGE ACROSS THE HEATER TO REACH 80% OF ITS RATED VOLTAGE AFTER APPLYING 4 TIMES RATED HEATER VOLTAGE TO A CIRCUIT CONSISTING OF THE TUBE HEATER IN SERIES WITH A RESISTANCE OF VALUE 3 TIMES THE NOMINAL HEATER OPERATING RESISTANCE.

CONTINUED ON FOLLOWING PAGE

12AT7
6201
ECC81

DOUBLE TRIODE
MINIATURE TYPE

COATED UNIPOTENTIAL CATHODES

HEATER

SERIES	PARALLEL
12.6 VOLTS	6.3 VOLTS
150 MA.	300 MA.

AC OR DC

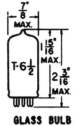

T-6½

GLASS BULB

FOR 12.6 VOLT OPERATION APPLY HEATER VOLTAGE BETWEEN PINS #4 AND #5. FOR 6.3 VOLT OPERATION APPLY HEATER VOLTAGE BETWEEN PIN #9 AND PINS #4 AND #5 CONNECTED TOGETHER.

ANY MOUNTING POSITION

BOTTOM VIEW
SMALL BUTTON
9 PIN BASE
9A

THE 12AT7 COMBINES TWO HIGH TRANSCONDUCTANCE TRIODES IN A 9 PIN MINIATURE CONSTRUCTION. ITS LOW CAPACITANCE AND HIGH RATIO OF PLATE CURRENT TO TRANSCONDUCTANCE ADAPT IT TO USE AS A HIGH FREQUENCY COMBINED OSCILLATOR AND MIXER OR AS A GROUNDED GRID RADIO FREQUENCY AMPLIFIER.

DIRECT INTERELECTRODE CAPACITANCES

	WITHOUT SHIELD	WITH SHIELD #316[A]	
INPUT: G TO (H+K) (EACH SECTION)	2.2	2.2	μμf
OUTPUT: P TO (H+K) (SECTION #1)	0.5	1.2	μμf
(SECTION #2)	0.4	1.5	μμf
GRID TO PLATE: (G TO P) (EACH SECTION)	1.5	1.5	μμf
HEATER TO CATHODE: (H TO K) (EACH SECTION)	2.4	2.4	μμf

GROUNDED GRID	WITHOUT SHIELD	WITH SHIELD #316[B]	
INPUT: K TO (H+G) (EACH SECTION)	4.6	4.6	μμf
OUTPUT: P TO (H+G) (EACH SECTION)	1.8	2.6	μμf
PLATE TO CATHODE (P TO K) (EACH SECTION)	0.2	0.2	μμf

[A] CONNECTED TO CATHODE OF SECTION UNDER TEST.

[B] CONNECTED TO GRID OF SECTION UNDER TEST.

RATINGS
INTERPRETED ACCORDING TO RMA STANDARD M8-210

EACH TRIODE UNIT

HEATER VOLTAGE	12.6	6.3	VOLTS
MAXIMUM HEATER—CATHODE VOLTAGE		90	VOLTS
MAXIMUM PLATE VOLTAGE		300	VOLTS
MAXIMUM NEGATIVE DC GRID VOLTAGE		-50	VOLTS
MAXIMUM PLATE DISSIPATION		2.5	WATTS

CONTINUED ON FOLLOWING PAGE

→ INDICATES A CHANGE OR ADDITION.

TWIN TRIODE
MINIATURE TYPE

12AU7A

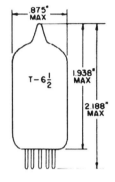

.875" MAX

1.938" MAX

2.188" MAX

T-6½

GLASS BULB
SMALL BUTTON NOVAL
9 PIN BASE E9-1
OUTLINE DRAWING
JEDEC 6-2

UNIPOTENTIAL CATHODE

FOR
AUDIO FREQUENCY AMPLIFIER
OR COMBINED OSCILLATOR AND
MIXER APPLICATIONS IN
T.V. RECEIVERS

ANY MOUNTING POSITION

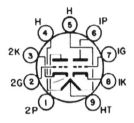

BOTTOM VIEW

BASING DIAGRAM
JEDEC 9A

THE 12AU7A COMBINES TWO INDEPENDENT MEDIUM-MU INDIRECTLY HEATED CATHODE TYPE TRIODES IN THE 9 PIN MINIATURE CONSTRUCTION. IT IS ADAPTABLE TO APPLICATION EITHER AS AN AUDIO FREQUENCY AMPLIFIER OR AS A COMBINED OSCILLATOR AND MIXER. EXCEPT FOR HEATER RATINGS IT IS IDENTICAL TO THE 7AU7 AND THE 9AU7.

→ DIRECT INTERELECTRODE CAPACITANCES

	TRIODE UNIT T_1	TRIODE UNIT T_2	
GRID TO PLATE	1.5	1.5	pf
GRID TO CATHODE	1.6	1.6	pf
PLATE TO CATHODE	0.50	0.35	pf

HEATER CHARACTERISTICS AND RATINGS
DESIGN MAXIMUM VALUES - SEE EIA STANDARD RS-239

AVERAGE CHARACTERISTICS			
HEATER IN SERIES	12.6 VOLTS	150	MA.
HEATER IN PARALLEL	6.3 VOLTS	300	MA.
HEATER SUPPLY LIMITS:			
VOLTAGE OPERATION			
HEATER IN SERIES		12.6±1.3	VOLTS
HEATER IN PARALLEL		6.3±0.6	VOLTS
MAXIMUM HEATER-CATHODE VOLTAGE:			
HEATER NEGATIVE WITH RESPECT TO CATHODE			
TOTAL DC AND PEAK		200	VOLTS
HEATER POSITIVE WITH RESPECT TO CATHODE			
DC		100	VOLTS
TOTAL DC AND PEAK		200	VOLTS

CONTINUED ON FOLLOWING PAGE

TUNG-SOL

TWIN TRIODE
MINIATURE TYPE

12AX7a
7025
ECC83

FOR

HIGH VOLTAGE GAIN AND

LOW HEATER POWER APPLICATIONS

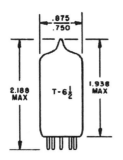

COATED UNIPOTENTIAL CATHODE

ANY MOUNTING POSITION

BOTTOM VIEW

BASING DIAGRAM
JEDEC 9A

GLASS BULB

SMALL BUTTON
9 PIN NOVAL E9-1
OUTLINE DRAWING
JEDEC 6-2

THE 12AX7A COMBINES TWO COMPLETELY INDEPENDENT HIGH-MU TRIODES IN THE 9 PIN MIN-
IATURE CONSTRUCTION. IT IS ADAPTABLE TO APPLICATIONS WHERE HIGH VOLTAGE GAIN AND
LOW HEATER POWER ARE THE IMPORTANT CONSIDERATIONS, AND IS SUITABLE FOR USE IN
MODERN HIGH GAIN AUDIO AMPLIFIERS AND MODERN TELEVISION CIRCUITS WHERE LOW HUM
AND LOW MICROPHONIC NOISE IS REQUIRED. THE CENTER TAPPED HEATER CONNECTION PER-
MITS OPERATION FROM EITHER A 6.3 VOLT OR 12.6 VOLT SUPPLY AND IN 300 MA. OR 150 MA.
SERIES HEATER SERVICE.

DIRECT INTERELECTRODE CAPACITANCES
WITHOUT EXTERNAL SHIELD

	TRIODE UNIT 1	TRIODE UNIT 2	
GRID TO PLATE	1.7	1.7	pf
GRID TO CATHODE	1.6	1.6	pf
PLATE TO CATHODE	0.46	0.34	pf

HEATER CHARACTERISTICS AND RATINGS
DESIGN MAXIMUM VALUES - SEE EIA STANDARD RS-239

SUPPLY CONNECTED TO PINS	4 AND 5	9 AND 4+5	
AVERAGE VALUES - VOLTAGE	12.6	6.3	VOLTS
CURRENT	150	300	MA.
HEATER WARM-UP TIME [A]		11	SECONDS
LIMITS OF APPLIED HEATER VOLTAGE	12.6 ±1.3	6.3 ±0.6	VOLTS
LIMITS OF SUPPLIED CURRENT	150± 10	300 ± 20	MA.
MAXIMUM PEAK HEATER-CATHODE VOLTAGE:			
HEATER NEGATIVE WITH RESPECT TO CATHODE		200	VOLTS
HEATER POSITIVE WITH RESPECT TO CATHODE		200 [A]	VOLTS

[A]THE DC COMPONENT MUST NOT EXCEET 100 VOLTS.

CONTINUED ON FOLLOWING PAGE

TUNG-SOL

12AY7

DOUBLE TRIODE

MINIATURE TYPE

COATED UNIPOTENTIAL CATHODE

HEATER

GLASS BULB

SERIES	PARALLEL
12.6 VOLTS	6.3 VOLTS
150 MA.	300 MA.

AC OR DC

FOR 12.6 VOLT OPERATION APPLY HEATER
VOLTAGE BETWEEN PINS #4 AND #5. FOR
6.3 VOLT OPERATION APPLY HEATER VOL-
TAGE BETWEEN PIN #9 AND PINS #4 AND
#5 CONNECTED TOGETHER.

WHEN OPERATING FROM AN AC HEATER SUP-
PLY, DO NOT USE THE 12.6 VOLT CONNEC-
TION IF LOW-HUM CAPABILITIES ARE TO
BE REALIZED.

ANY MOUNTING POSITION

BOTTOM VIEW
SMALL BUTTON
9 PIN BASE
9A

THE 12AY7 COMBINES TWO INDEPENDENT MEDIUM-MU INDIRECTLY HEATED CATHODE
TYPE TRIODES IN THE SMALL 9 PIN BUTTON MINIATURE CONSTRUCTION. IT IS IN-
TENDED FOR USE IN HIGH GAIN AUDIO AMPLIFIER SERVICE WHERE PARTICULAR
ATTENTION IS PAID TO MICROPHONICS, HUM, AND OTHER SOURCES OF INTERNAL
NOISE.

DIRECT INTERELECTRODE CAPACITANCES - APPROX.
WITH NO EXTERNAL SHIELD

	EACH UNIT	
GRID TO PLATE: (G TO P)	1.3	$\mu\mu f$
INPUT: G TO (H+K)	1.3	$\mu\mu f$
OUTPUT: P TO (H+K)	0.6	$\mu\mu f$

RATINGS
INTERPRETED ACCORDING TO DESIGN CENTER SYSTEM

EACH TRIODE UNIT

HEATER VOLTAGE	12.6	6.3	VOLTS
MAXIMUM DC HEATER-CATHODE VOLTAGE	90		VOLTS
MAXIMUM PLATE DISSIPATION	1.5		WATTS
MAXIMUM CATHODE CURRENT	10		MA.

TYPICAL OPERATING CONDITIONS AND CHARACTERISTICS
CLASS A AMPLIFIER

EACH TRIODE UNIT

HEATER VOLTAGE	12.6	6.3	VOLTS
HEATER CURRENT	150	300	MA.
PLATE VOLTAGE	250		VOLTS
GRID VOLTAGE	-4		VOLTS
PLATE CURRENT	3		MA.
TRANSCONDUCTANCE	1 750		μMHOS
AMPLIFICATION FACTOR	44		
PLATE RESISTANCE (APPROX.)	25 000		OHMS

CONTINUED ON FOLLOWING PAGE

TUNG-SOL

12DW7

DOUBLE TRIODE
MINIATURE TYPE

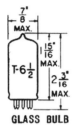

COATED UNIPOTENTIAL CATHODE

HEATER

SERIES	PARALLEL
12.6 VOLTS	6.3 VOLTS
0.15 AMP.	0.30 AMP.

AC OR DC

ANY MOUNTING POSITION

GLASS BULB

BOTTOM VIEW
SMALL BUTTON
9 PIN BASE

9 A

THE 12DW7 IS A DISSIMILAR DOUBLE TRIODE IN THE 9 PIN MINIATURE CONSTRUCTION. IT IS ESPECIALLY SUITABLE FOR APPLICATIONS REQUIRING A HIGH GAIN VOLTAGE AMPLIFIER AND A CATHODYNE TYPE PHASE-INVERTER.

DIRECT INTERELECTRODE CAPACITANCES

	SECTION #1 [A]		SECTION #2 [A]		
	WITH [B] SHIELD	WITHOUT SHIELD	WITH [B] SHIELD	WITHOUT SHIELD	
GRID TO PLATE	1.7	1.7	1.5	1.5	$\mu\mu f$
INPUT: G TO (H + K)	1.8	1.6	1.8	1.7	$\mu\mu f$
OUTPUT: P TO(H + K)	2.0	0.44	2.4	0.4	$\mu\mu f$

RATINGS
INTERPRETED ACCORDING TO DESIGN MAXIMUM SYSTEM [C]

	SECTION #1	SECTION #2	
HEATER VOLTAGE (SERIES)		12.6	VOLTS
HEATER VOLTAGE (PARALLEL)		6.3	VOLTS
MAXIMUM PLATE VOLTAGE	330	330	VOLTS
MAXIMUM PLATE DISSIPATION	1.2	3.3	WATT
MAXIMUM CATHODE CURRENT	---	22	MA.
MAXIMUM POSITIVE DC GRID VOLTAGE	0	---	VOLTS
MAXIMUM NEGATIVE DC GRID VOLTAGE	55	---	VOLTS
MAXIMUM GRID CIRCUIT RESISTANCE:			
FIXED BIAS		0.25	MEGOHM
SELF BIAS		1.0	MEGOHM
MAXIMUM HEATER-CATHODE VOLTAGE:			
HEATER NEGATIVE WITH RESPECT TO CATHODE			
TOTAL DC AND PEAK		200	VOLTS
HEATER POSITIVE WITH RESPECT TO CATHODE			
DC		100	VOLTS
TOTAL DC AND PEAK		200	VOLTS

CONTINUED ON FOLLOWING PAGE

BEAM PENTODE

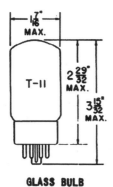

COATED UNIPOTENTIAL CATHODE

HEATER

6.3 VOLTS   0.9 AMP.

AC OR DC

ANY MOUNTING POSITION

BOTTOM VIEW

SHORT INTERMEDIATE
SHELL 7 PIN OCTAL

7AC

T-11

1 7/16" MAX.

2 29/32" MAX.

3 15/32" MAX.

GLASS BULB

THE 5881 IS THE ELECTRICAL EQUIVALENT TO TYPES 6L6 AND 6L6G EXCEPT THAT THE PLATE AND SCREEN DISSIPATION RATINGS HAVE BEEN INCREASED APPROXIMATELY 20 PERCENT. IT EMBODIES A COMPLETE MECHANICAL REDESIGN WHICH RESULTS IN GREATER RESISTANCE TO SHOCK AND VIBRATION. THE USE OF TREATED GRIDS AND ANODE GREATLY INCREASES ITS OVERLOAD CAPABILITIES AND THEREBY PROVIDES DESIRABLE IMPROVEMENT IN CONTINUITY OF SERVICE. THE ADDITION OF A LOW-LOSS BARRIER TYPE BASE WILL PROVIDE OBVIOUS ADVANTAGES IN CERTAIN APPLICATIONS.

RATINGS
INTERPRETED ACCORDING TO RMA STANDARD M8-210

HEATER VOLTAGE	6.3	VOLTS
MAXIMUM HEATER-CATHODE VOLTAGE	200	VOLTS
MAXIMUM PLATE VOLTAGE	400	VOLTS
MAXIMUM GRID #2 VOLTAGE	400	VOLTS
MAXIMUM PLATE VOLTAGE (TRIODE CONNECTION)	400	VOLTS
MAXIMUM PLATE DISSIPATION	23	WATTS
MAXIMUM GRID #2 DISSIPATION	3	WATTS
MAXIMUM PLATE DISSIPATION (TRIODE CONNECTION)	26	WATTS
MAXIMUM GRID RESISTANCE (FIXED BIAS)	0.1	MEGOHM
MAXIMUM GRID RESISTANCE (SELF BIAS)	0.5	MEGOHM

TYPICAL OPERATING CONDITIONS AND CHARACTERISTICS

CLASS A$_1$ AMPLIFIER - SINGLE TUBE

HEATER VOLTAGE	6.3	6.3	6.3	VOLTS
HEATER CURRENT	0.9	0.9	0.9	AMP.
PLATE VOLTAGE	250	300	350	VOLTS
GRID #2 VOLTAGE	250	200	250	VOLTS
GRID #1 VOLTAGE	-14	-12.5	-18	VOLTS
PEAK AF SIGNAL VOLTAGE	14	12.5	18	VOLTS
TRANSCONDUCTANCE	6 100	5 300	5 200	μMHOS
PLATE RESISTANCE	30 000	35 000	48 000	OHMS
ZERO-SIGNAL PLATE CURRENT	75	48	53	MA.
ZERO-SIGNAL GRID #2 CURRENT	4.3	2.5	2.5	MA.
MAXIMUM SIGNAL PLATE CURRENT	80	55	65	MA.
MAXIMUM SIGNAL GRID #2 CURRENT	7.6	4.7	8.5	MA.
LOAD RESISTANCE	2 500	4 500	4 200	OHMS
POWER OUTPUT	6.7	6.5	11.3	WATTS
TOTAL HARMONIC DISTORTION	10	11	13	PERCENT

CONTINUED ON FOLLOWING PAGE

➤ INDICATES A CHANGE OR ADDITION.

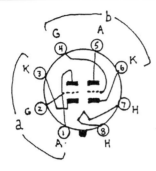

LOW-MU
DUAL-POWER TRIODE

6080WA
6080
6AS7G

Glass octal-type used as a regulator tube in DC power supplies. May be mounted in any position with adequate ventilation.

Physical:	Maximum overall length	103mm
	Maximum seated height	89mm
	Diameter	44mm

Heater Requirements: 6.3V AC or DC
2,500 mA

Maximum Ratings	V_A	250	V
(per section):	P_A	13	W
	I_A	125	mA
	$V_{H \cdot K}$	300	V
	μ	2	

Maximum Circuit Values: R_{G1} 100kΩ, for fixed-bias operation
1MΩ, for cathode-bias operation

—PRODUCT INFORMATION—

ELECTRONIC
INNOVATIONS
IN ACTION

TUBES

Beam Pentode

6550-A

FOR AF POWER-AMPLIFIER APPLICATIONS

- AUDIO POWER OUTPUT
- UP TO 100 WATTS OUTPUT - 2 TUBES IN PUSH-PULL
- 42 WATTS PLATE DISSIPATION

The 6550-A is a beam-power pentode primarily designed for use in audio-frequency power-amplifier applications. It carries a 42 watt plate dissipation rating which provides for push-pull amplifier designs up to 100 watts output.

The 6550-A features a straight sided T-14 envelope and may be used as a direct replacement for the 6550.

GENERAL

ELECTRICAL

Cathode - Coated Unipotential

Heater Characteristics and Ratings
Heater Voltage, AC or DC .... 6.3±0.6 Volts
Heater Current .... 1.6 Amperes
Direct interelectrode Capacitances:
  Grid-Number 1 to Plate: (g1 to p) .... 0.8 pf
  input: g1 to (h – k – g2 – b.p.) .... 15 pf
  Output: p to (h – k – g2 – b.p.) .... 10 pf

MECHANICAL

Mounting Position - Any
Envelope - T-14, Glass
Base - B7-99, Large-Wafer Octal with Sleeve Low Loss 7-Pin Micanol
Outline Drawing - EIA 14-16
  Maximum Diameter .... 1.813 Inches
  Minimum Bulb Diameter .... 1.687 Inches
  Maximum Over-all Length .... 4.562 Inches
  Maximum Seated Height .... 4.000 Inches
  Minimum Seated Height .... 3.750 Inches

PHYSICAL DIMENSIONS

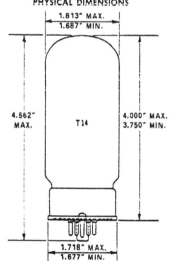

1.813" MAX.
1.687" MIN.

4.562" MAX.
T14
4.000" MAX.
3.750" MIN.

1.718" MAX.
1.677" MIN.

EIA 14-16

TERMINAL CONNECTIONS

Pin 1 - No Connection or Base Shell
Pin 2 - Heater
Pin 3 - Plate
Pin 4 - Grid-Number 2 (Screen)
Pin 5 - Grid-Number 1
Pin 7 - Heater
Pin 8 - Cathode and Beam Plates

BASING DIAGRAM

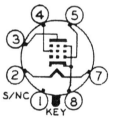

S/NC
KEY

EIA 7AC

MAXIMUM RATINGS

DESIGN-MAXIMUM VALUES

	Pentode Connection	Triode Connection ♦	
DC Plate Voltage	660	500	Volts
DC Screen Voltage	440 §	– – –	Volts
Positive DC Grid-Number 1 Voltage	0	0	Volts
Negative DC Grid-Number 1 Voltage	300	300	Volts
Plate Dissipation	42	42	Watts
Screen Dissipation (Average)	6.0	– – –	Watts
Screen Dissipation (Peak)	10	– – –	Watts
DC Cathode Current	190	190	Milliamperes
Heater-Cathode Voltage			
Heater Positive with Respect to Cathode			
DC Component	100	100	Volts
Total DC and Peak	200	200	Volts
Heater Negative with Respect to Cathode			
Total DC and Peak	300	300	Volts
Grid-Number 1 Circuit Resistance			
With Fixed Bias	0.05	0.05	Megohms
With Cathode Bias	0.25	0.25	Megohms
Bulb Temperature at Hottest Point ⊕	250	250	°C

Design-Maximum ratings are limiting values of operating and environmental conditions applicable to a bogey electron tube of a specified type as defined by its published data and should not be exceeded under the worst probable conditions.

The tube manufacturer chooses these values to provide acceptable serviceability of the tube, making allowance for the effects of changes in operating conditions due to variations in the characteristics of the tube under consideration.

The equipment manufacturer should design so that initially and throughout life no design-maximum value for the intended service is exceeded with a bogey tube under the worst probable operating conditions with respect to supply-voltage variation, equipment component variation, equipment control adjustment, load variation, signal variation, environmental conditions, and variations in the characteristics of all other electron devices in the equipment.

CHARACTERISTICS AND TYPICAL OPERATION

AVERAGE CHARACTERISTICS, PENTODE CONNECTION

Plate Voltage	250	Volts
Screen Voltage	250	Volts
Grid-Number 1 Voltage	–14	Volts
Plate Current	140	Milliamperes
Screen Current	12	Milliamperes
Transconductance	11,000	Micromhos
Plate Resistance, approximate	15,000	Ohms
Triode Amplification Factor	8	
Grid-Number 1 Voltage		
Ib = 1.0 Milliamperes	–40	Volts

CLASS A, AUDIO-AMPLIFIER, SINGLE TUBE

DC Plate Voltage	250	400	Volts
DC Screen Voltage	250	225	Volts
DC Grid-Number 1 Voltage	–14	–16.5	Volts
Peak AF Grid-Number 1 Voltage	14	16.5	Volts
Zero-Signal DC Plate Current	140	87	Milliamperes
Maximum-Signal DC Plate Current	150	105	Milliamperes
Zero-Signal DC Screen Current	12	4.0	Milliamperes
Maximum-Signal DC Screen Current	22	14	Milliamperes
Load Resistance	1,500	3,000	Ohms
Total Harmonic Distortion	7	13.5	Percent
Maximum-Signal Power Output	12.5	20	Watts

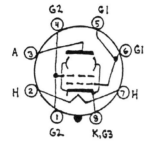

G2 G1
A G1
H H
G2 K,G3

BEAM POWER   7027A
PENTODE

Glass octal type used in output stage of low-distortion audio frequency amplifiers.

Should be mounted vertically with adequate ventilation provided.

Physical: Maximum overall length   118mm
Maximum seated height   104mm
Diameter   42mm

Heater Requirements: 6.3V AC or DC
900 mA

Maximum Ratings:

V_A	600	V
V_{G2}	500	V
P_A	35	W
P_{G2}	5	W
I_A	150	mA
g_m	5	mS

Maximum Circuit Values: R_{G1} 100kΩ, for fixed-bias operation
500kΩ, for cathode-bias operation

PENTODE PUSH-PULL

	SELF-BIAS	ULTRA-LINEAR	FIXED-BIAS	
V_A	400	410	450	V
V_{G2}	300	U.L.	350	V
R_{G2} (common)	—	—	—	Ω
I_A (0)	2x56	2x67	2x47	mA
I_A (max. sig.)	2x54	2x77	2x92	mA
I_{G2} (0)	2x3.5	----	2x1.7	mA
I_{G2} (max. sig.)	2x3	—	2x9.6	mA
R_K	200	220	—	Ω
R_{A-A}	6.6	8	6	kΩ
V_{G1}	-23	-30	-30	V
V_{IN} (g-g) (pp)	46	60	60	V
P_{OUT}	32	24	50	W
D_{TOT}	5	2	8	%

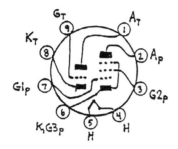

MEDIUM-MU TRIODE   7199
SHARP-CUTOFF PENTODE

Miniature 9-pin type combining a triode section optimixed for phase-splitter use, and a pentode intended for high-fidelity audio frequency voltage amplifiers.

Tube is optimized for low microphony and low hum.

Physical:

Maximum overall length	56mm
Maximum seated height	49mm
Diameter	22mm

Heater Requirements: 6.3V AC or DC
                                 450mA

Maximum Ratings:

	Triode section	Pentode section	
V_A	330	330	V
V_{G2}	----	330	V
P_A	2.4	3.0	W
P_{G2}	----	0.6	W
I_A	9	13	mA
V_{H-K}	200	200	V
μ	17	----	
e_n	10	35	μV

Pentode Section V+ = 300V

R_A (kΩ)	R_L (kΩ)	R_K (Ω)	E_{OUT}	A_V
220	220	9k20	52	182
220	470	1k10	66	236
220	1M	1k20	77	357
470	470	1k95	41	221
470	1M	3k21	72	296
470	2M2	2k20	82	345
1M	1M	4k10	57	295
1M	2M2	4k34	74	378

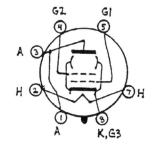

BEAM POWER PENTODE   8417

Glass octal-type used as output of high-fidelity, high-power audio frequency amplifiers. May be supplied with pin 6 omitted.

May be mounted in any position with adequate ventilation provided.

Physical:	Maximum overall length	114mm
	Maximum seated height	99mm
	Diameter	40mm

Heater Requirements:	6.3V AC or DC
	1,600 mA

Maximum Ratings:

V_A	660	V
V_{G2}	500	V
P_A	35	W
P_{G2}	8	W
I_A	200	mA
g_m	23	mS

Maximum Circuit Values: R_{G1} 100kΩ, for fixed-bias operation
250kΩ, for cathode-bias operation

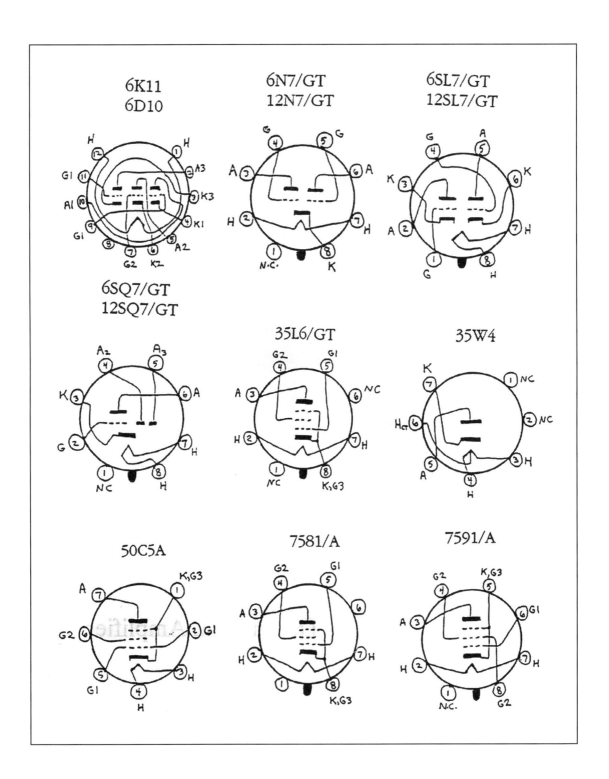

MULTI-ELECTRODE TUBES were developed to extend the capability of conventional tubes. In some cases, a multi-element tube may contain up to seven grids. These types of tubes are normally classified by the number of grids they contain.

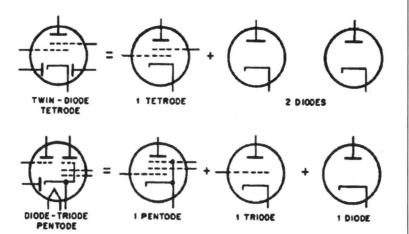

POWER PENTODES are used as current or power amplifiers. Power pentodes use in-line grid arrangements. In this manner, more electrons can reach the plate from the cathode. In effect, this lowers plate resistance and allows maximum conduction through the tube.

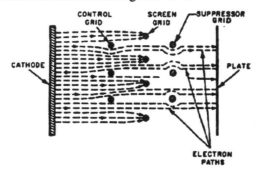

SYMBOLS OF TUBE ELEMENTS

USE THIS COLUMN FOR ALL DATA SHEETS DATED PRIOR TO JUNE 15, 1944		USE THIS COLUMN FOR ALL DATA SHEETS DATED JUNE 15, 1944 AND LATER	
G_a	Anode Grid	A (A_1, A_2, etc.)	Anode
R	Ray Control Electrode	D (D_1, D_2, etc.)	Deflectors, Ray Control Electrode
F	Filament	F	Filament
F_t	Filament Tap	F_t	Filament Tap
G	Control Grid	G (G_1, G_2, etc.)	Grid
H	Heater	H	Heater
H_t	Heater Tap	H_t	Heater Tap
I_c	Internal Connection	I_c	Internal Connection (Not For External Use)
		J	Jumper
K	Cathode	K	Cathode
N_c	No Connection	N_c	No Connection
P	Plate	P (P_1, P_2, etc.)	Plate, Diode Plate
D_p	Diode Plate		
S	Metal Shell	S	Shell
S_i	Internal Shield	S_i	Internal Shield
X_s	External Shield	S_x	External Shield
T	Target	T	Target
▮	Beam Plate	▮	Beam Plate
F_c	Filament Center (Electrical)		
G_m	Modulator Grid		
G_o	Oscillator Grid		
G_s	Screen Grid		
H_c	Heater Center (Electrical)		
P_i	Input Plate		
P_o	Oscillator Plate		
P_r	Remote Cut-Off Plate		
P_s	Sharp Cut-Off Plate		
S_u	Suppressor Grid		

▲ GRID SUBSCRIPT NUMBERS ARE USED ONLY WHEN THERE IS MORE THAN ONE GRID IN THE TUBE. THEY SIGNIFY THE SEQUENCE FROM THE CATHODE. FOR EXAMPLE, G_3 INDICATES THE 3RD. GRID FROM THE CATHODE. WHEN THERE ARE TWIN ELEMENTS IN A TUBE, SUBSCRIPTS ARE USED ONLY IF THERE IS MORE THAN ONE GRID IN ANY GIVEN UNIT. FOR EXAMPLE, A TRIODE-PENTODE IS LABELLED G_2, G_3 FOR A PENTODE SECTION, WHEREAS THE TRIODE SECTION IS LABELLED G. IF THERE ARE 2 PENTODE SECTIONS, THERE ARE THEN TWO SETS OF SUBSCRIPTS.

European Tube Nomenclature

The first letter is the heater current or voltage.

A	=	4 V
E	=	6.3 V
D	=	1.4 V
G	=	5 V
H	=	150 ma. Series
K	=	2 V
P	=	300 ma Series
U	=	100 ma Series
V	=	50 ma Series
Q	=	Tetrode

The second letter is what type of tube it is.

A	=	Diode
B	=	Double Diode
C	=	Triode
D	=	Tetrode
F	=	Pentode
H	=	Heptode
L	=	Pentode
M	=	Tuning Indicator
Y	=	Rectifier
Z	=	Rectifier

The third letter indicates whether the tube has double or more functions. This letter has the same meaning as the second. ECC83 means 6.3 V triode, EBF80 means 6.3 V double diode pentode.

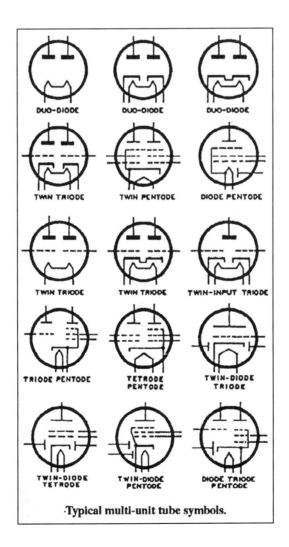

·Typical multi-unit tube symbols.

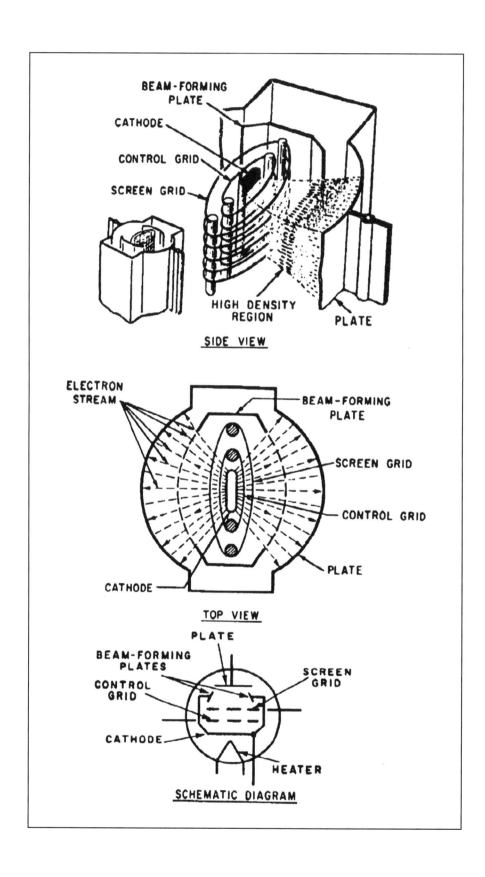

BEAM-FORMING PLATE

CATHODE

CONTROL GRID

SCREEN GRID

HIGH DENSITY REGION

PLATE

SIDE VIEW

ELECTRON STREAM

BEAM-FORMING PLATE

SCREEN GRID

CONTROL GRID

PLATE

CATHODE

TOP VIEW

PLATE

BEAM-FORMING PLATES

CONTROL GRID

SCREEN GRID

CATHODE

HEATER

SCHEMATIC DIAGRAM

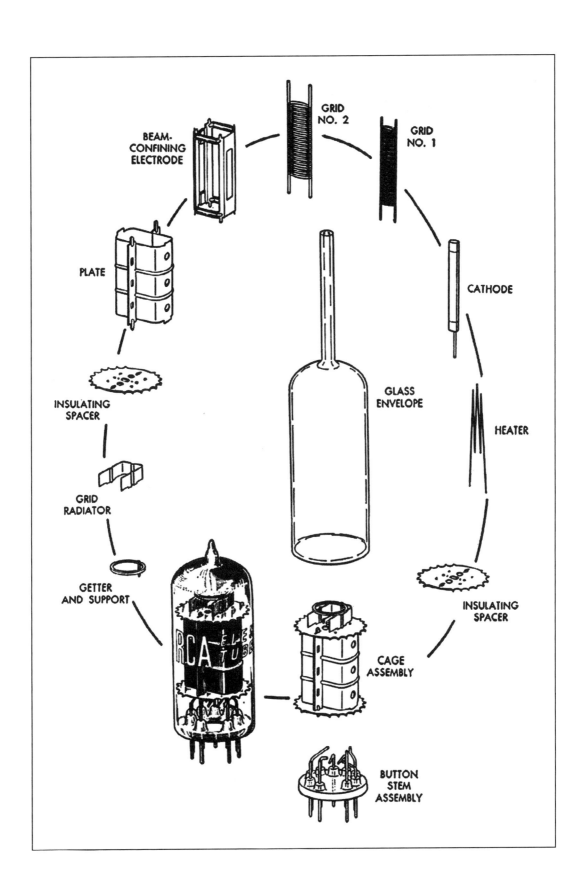

BEAM-CONFINING ELECTRODE

GRID NO. 2

GRID NO. 1

PLATE

CATHODE

INSULATING SPACER

GLASS ENVELOPE

HEATER

GRID RADIATOR

GETTER AND SUPPORT

INSULATING SPACER

CAGE ASSEMBLY

BUTTON STEM ASSEMBLY

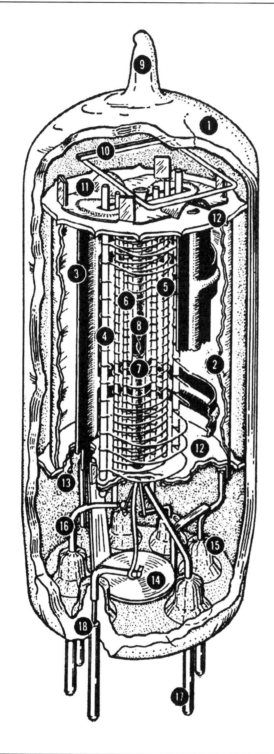

1—Glass Envelope

2—Internal Shield

3—Plate

4—Grid No. 3 (Suppressor)

5—Grid No. 2 (Screen)

6—Grid No. 1 (Control Grid)

7—Cathode

8—Heater

9—Exhaust Tip

10—Getter

11—Spacer Shield Header

12—Insulating Spacer

13—Spacer Shield

14—Inter-Pin Shield

15—Glass Button-Stem Seal

16—Lead Wire

17—Base Pin

18—Glass-to-Metal Seal

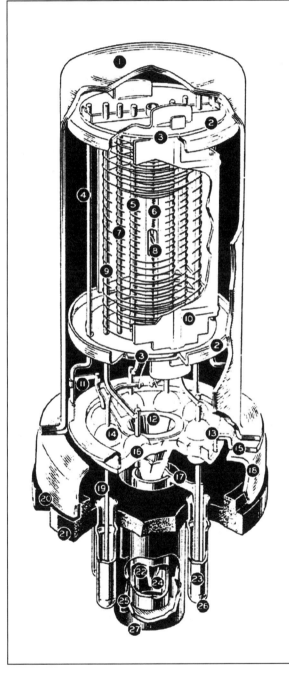

1—METAL ENVELOPE
2—SPACER SHIELD
3—INSULATING SPACER
4—MOUNT SUPPORT
5—CONTROL GRID
6—COATED CATHODE
7—SCREEN
8—HEATER
9—SUPPRESSOR
10—PLATE
11—BATALUM GETTER
12—CONICAL STEM SHIELD
13—HEATER INSERT
14—GLASS SEAL
15—HEADER
16—GLASS-BUTTON STEM SEAL
17—CYLINDER BASE SHIELD
18—HEADER SKIRT
19—LEAD WIRE
20—CRIMPED LOCK
21—OCTAL BASE
22—EXHAUST TUBE
23—BASE PIN
24—EXHAUST TIP
25—ALIGNING KEY
26—SOLDER
27—ALIGNING PLUG

A Glossary of Amplifier Terminology

Accelerating Anode—An electrode charged to several thousand volts positive and used to accelerate electrons toward the front of a cathode-ray tube.

Acorn Tube—A very small tube with closely spaced electrodes and no base. The tube is connected to its circuits by short wire pins that are sealed in a glass or ceramic envelope. The acorn tube is used in low-power UHF circuits.

ADSR—It stands for *attack, decay, sustain, release,* which is the most general way to describe a musical envelope. This is terminology borrowed from the synthesizer folks.

Amperite (Ballast) Tube—A current-controlling resistance device designed to maintain substantially constant current over a specified range of variation in applied voltage or resistance of a series circuit.

Amplification—The ratio of output magnitude to input magnitude in a device intended to produce an output that is an enlarged reproduction of its input.

Amplification Factor—The voltage gain of an amplifier with no load on the output. It is the ratio of a small change in plate voltage to a small change in control-grid voltage under the conditions that the plate current remains unchanged and that all other electrode voltages are maintained at a constant level. It is a measure of the effectiveness of the control-grid voltage relative to that of the plate voltage upon the plate current.

Amplitude Distortion—Results from non-linear amplification in such a manner that the output waveform is not exactly proportional to the amplitude of the input signal; harmonics of the signal are generated in the amplifier. It is distortion that is present in an amplifier when the amplitude of the output signal fails to follow exactly any increase or decrease in the amplitude of the input signal.

Anode—A positive electrode of an electrochemical device (such as a secondary or primary cell) toward which negative ions are drawn.

Aquadag Coating—A special coating of a conductive material, such as graphite, which is applied to the inside of a cathode ray tube. This coating eliminates the effects of secondary emission and aids in the acceleration of electrons.

Arbitrary Waveform Generation—This effect generates a completely new waveform of arbitrary shape, which shares the same frequency as the input waveform. Guitar synthesizers do a version of this.

Asymmetrical Clipping—Occurs when the top or bottom half of a waveform is clipped more than the other half. This causes the generation of both even and odd harmonics, in contrast to symmetrical clipping's odd order only. The even harmonics are smoother and more musical sounding, and not as harsh as the odd ones. The hardness of clipping and the degree of asymmetry affect the sound. The more asymmetry, the more pronounced the even-order harmonics, the harsher the clipping, and the more the harmonics are skewed toward higher order.

Asymmetrical Compression—Occurs when only the peaks of the input waveforms are compressed, not the overall level of the waveform envelope. Effectively, there is no averaging of the envelope and the instantaneous waveform level is compressed. This amounts to a much softer form of clipping, and is part of the tube sound. Tubes with a soft B+ supply are prone to this.

Attack Delay—A variation of noise gating where the transition from "off" to "on" or no signal state is slowed. This gives an output that perceptibly rises in level with each new note envelope. It is reminiscent of a tape recording played backwards.

Auto Swell—A rise in level from a starting level to a final level when keyed manually or electronically. This can effectively add sustain to some notes and not to others when keyed manually, add a swell in volume over a run of notes, or help with presetting the level of a lead.

Auto Tremolo—Tremolo where the modulation frequency is varied by some feature of the input signal, generally amplitude. See **Tremolo.**

Auto Wah (Envelope Follower)—A wah filter where the center frequency is determined by the loudness of the input signal, making a moving resonance on every note. See **Wah.**

Beam Power Tube—An electron tube in which the grids are aligned with the control grid. Special beam-forming plates are used to concentrate the electron stream into the beam. Because of this action, the beam power tube has high power-handling capabilities.

Brightness Control—The name given to the potentiometer used to vary the potential applied to the control grid of a cathode ray tube.

Bus—A bus electrical work is a piece of copper or aluminum wire used to connect all collective fuses to the main power. A mixer has several buses to assign the signal from an individual channel to other grouped areas.

Cabinet Simulator—A filter network designed to mimic the two- or four-pole low- and high-frequency rolloff of a guitar speaker cabinet in order to create the sound of a speaker cabinet being close-miked.

Cathode—The general name for any negative electrode.

Cathode Bias—The method of biasing a vacuum tube by placing the biasing resistor in the common cathode return circuit, thereby making the cathode more positive with respect to ground.

Cathode Current—The total electronic current passing to or from the cathode through the vacuous space.

Cathode Ray Tube (CRT)—An electron tube that has an electron gun, a deflection system, and a screen. This type of tube is used to display visual electronic signals.

Choke—An inductor used to impede the flow of pulsating DC or AC by means of self-inductance.

Class A Amplifier—An amplifier in which the grid bias and the exciting grid voltage are such that plate current flows approximately 360 degrees of the cycle. The ideal Class A amplifier operates on the linear portion of the plate current versus the grid voltage characteristic in such a manner that the waveform of the plate current is an exact reproduction of the exciting grid voltage. A Class A amplifier is characterized by low efficiency, low output, and low harmonic distortion.

Class AB Amplifier—An amplifier in which the grid bias and the exciting grid voltage are such that plate current flows for appreciably more than 180 electrical degrees but less than 360 electrical degrees of the cycle. This class of amplifier, sometimes designated as a Class A (Prime) amplifier, is characterized by efficiency, output, and percentage of harmonic distortion intermediate to those of Class A and Class B amplifiers.

Class B Amplifier—An amplifier in which the grid bias and the exciting grid voltage are such that plate current flows approximately 180 electrical degrees of the cycle. The grid bias is approximately equal to the plate current cut-off value, and the power output is proportional to the square of the excitation grid voltage. A Class B amplifier is characterized by medium efficiency, medium output, and medium percentage of harmonic distortion.

Class BC Amplifier—Is an amplifier in which the grid bias and the exciting grid voltage are such that the plate current flows slightly less than 180 electrical degrees of the cycle. A Class BC Amplifier is characterized by efficiency, output, and percentage of harmonic distortion intermediate to those of Class B and Class C amplifiers.

Class C Amplifier—An amplifier in which the grid bias and the exciting grid voltage are such that the plate current flows for considerably fewer electrical degrees of the cycle. A Class C amplifier is characterized by high plate circuit efficiency, high power output, and a high percentage of harmonic distortion.

Cold Cathode Tube—A gas-filled electron tube that conducts without the use of filaments. Cold cathode tubes are used as voltage regulators.

Compression—An effect that makes soft inputs louder and loud ones softer, giving a "one-level" kind of sound with lessened dynamics. This is an effective volume control with the level determined by the negation of the averaged envelope of the input level. Early compressors were often called *sustain pedals*.

Control Gain—The ratio of the magnitude of the intermediate frequency voltage developed at the output circuit of the frequency converter, to the magnitude of the exciting voltage applied to the signal grid.

Control Grid—The electrode of a vacuum tube, other than a diode, upon which a signal voltage is impressed to regulate the plate current.

Conversion Plate Impedance—The ratio of a small change in the plate voltage of a frequency converter to a small change in its plate current under the conditions that all direct voltages remain constant and that no impedances to the oscillator frequency or to the measurement frequency are present in its plate circuit.

Conversion Transconductance—The ratio of a small magnitude of the single-beat frequency component of the output electrode current to the magnitude of the small control electrode voltage of frequency. This is under the conditions that all direct electrode voltages and the magnitude of the electrode alternating voltage remain constant and that no impedances at the frequencies are present in the output circuit.

Crossover—Allows a certain frequency range to be sent to a specific driver. There are two types of crossovers commonly used: a passive or high-level crossover and an active or electronic crossover.

Cross Modulation—The modulation of the carrier of the desired signal by the modulation of the voltage of an undesired signal.

Current—All substances are made up of atoms and each atom consists of tiny particles called electrons. The electrons in some atoms are very stable, while in other materials they are unstable. Electrons in less stable atoms can be made to jump from one atom to another. Materials that will give up electrons easily in this manner are known as *conductors*. The movement of electrons is called *current flow*. This flow of current is rated in amperes or amps.

Damping Factor—The rated load impedance divided by the sum of the internal output impedance of the amplifier and the DC resistance of the voice coil. It refers to the ability of an amplifier to control precisely a speaker's movement. Generally, the higher the number, the greater the control the amp has over the speaker and, therefore, the more accurate the response.

DBu—Since dB can be used to measure voltage, a common scale in matching equipment is called dBu where 0 dBu is referenced to .775 V. This number is commonly found in reference to sound reinforcement equipment. When a mixer produces one milliwatt of power (1/1000 watt) into 600 ohms, the voltage level is .775 V. This stems back to the phone company and the impedance of telephones.

DBV—Is used for voltage comparison. Voltage ratios are based on 6 dB equaling twice the voltage, instead of our power ratio where 3 dB equals twice the power.

Deflection Plates—Two pairs of parallel electrodes, one pair set forward (in front of) of the other and at right angles to each other, parallel to the axis of the electron stream within an electrostatic cathode ray tube.

Deionization Potential—The potential at which ionization of the gas within a gas-filled tube ceases and the conduction stops; also referred to as the *extinction potential.*

Demodulation—The process of recovering a modulating signal in a detector from a modulated wave.

Difference of Potential—The voltage existing between two points. This results in a flow of electrons whenever a circuit is established between the two points.

Diode—An electron tube containing two electrodes, a cathode, and a plate. There are other diodes called *semiconductor diodes*. Older diodes were made of selenium, whereas newer diodes are made of silicon. In the schematic symbol for the diode, the triangle is the plate or anode and the crossbar is the cathode. Voltage drop across silicon diodes is much smaller than that across selenium diodes.

Direct Radiators—A speaker that propagates sound directly into the listening area. There are no other acoustic elements between the speaker and the ear other than the air itself. By using a baffle, several benefits can be obtained—one is that because phase problems are eliminated, better low-frequency response can be obtained.

Directivity—The frequency response throughout a certain dispersion pattern. High directivity signifies a narrow dispersion pattern and, generally, a short throw.

Directly-Heated Cathode—A wire or filament designed to emit electrons that flow from cathode to plate. This is accomplished by passing a current through the filament; the current heats the filament to the point where electrons are emitted.

Doorknob Tube—An electron tube that is similar to the acorn tube but larger. The doorknob tube is designed to operate at high power in the UHF frequencies.

Edison Effect—The phenomenon wherein electrons emitted from a heated element within a vacuum tube will flow to a second element that is connected to a positive potential. It's also called the *Richardson Effect*.

Electron Gun—An electrode of a CRT that is equivalent to the cathode and control grid of a conventional tube. An electron gun produces a highly concentrated stream of electrons.

Electrostatic Deflection—The method of deflecting an electron beam by passing it between parallel charged plates mounted inside a cathode ray tube.

Enhancers—These split a signal into several bands, slightly distort some of the bands, and then remix them.

Ep-Ip Curve—The characteristic curve of an electron tube used to graphically depict the relationship between plate voltage (Ep) and plate current (Ip).

Expansion—Makes loud sounds louder and soft ones softer. Effectively, it's volume control with the level determined by the averaged envelope of the input level. Compression and expansion can be complementary as, for instance, when used for noise reduction.

Filament—The cathode of a thermionic tube—usually a wire or ribbon—which is heated by passing current through it.

Filter—A selective network of resistors, capacitors, and inductors that offers comparatively little opposition to certain frequencies, or to direct current while blocking or attenuating other frequencies.

Fixed Bias—A constant value of bias voltage.

Fleming Valve—An earlier name for a diode, or a two-electrode vacuum tube used as a detector.

Focusing Anode—An electrode of a CRT that is used to focus electrons into a tight beam.

Frequency Distortion—Results when the frequency components of an input signal are not amplified with equal magnitude.

Frequency Response—The frequency response measurement is made by sweeping a waveform throughout the entire spectrum and plotting it on a graph. The frequency response of an amplifier should be as flat as possible throughout the entire audio spectrum, 20 Hz to 20 KHz. Many amplifier companies publish responses that range from 5 Hz to 50 KHz.

Full-Wave Rectifier—A circuit that uses both positive and negative alternations in an alternating current to produce direct current.

Getter—An alkali metal introduced inside a vacuum tube during manufacture. It is fired after the tube has been evacuated to react chemically with and eliminate any remaining gases.

Grid Bias—A constant potential applied between the grid and cathode of a vacuum tube to establish an operating point.

Grid Current—The current that flows in the grid to the cathode circuit of a vacuum tube.

Grid-Leak Bias—A high resistance connected across a grid capacitor or between a grid and cathode. It provides a DC path to limit the accumulation of a charge on a grid.

Half-Wave Rectifier—A rectifier using only one half of each cycle to change AC to pulsating DC. In audio circuits, this produces a prominent second harmonic, heard as an octave. Half-wave rectification represents the logical conclusion of asymmetrical clipping.

Harmonics—A complex tone can be characterized as two or more waves having different frequencies, amplitudes, and phase relationships. Waves that have frequencies related by whole numbers are called harmonics.

Harmonic Distortion—When an amplifier is at full power, there is typically a slight alteration of the output signal comparative to the input signal; this is caused by the amplifier producing a certain percentage of harmonics along with the original signal. These harmonics are "ghost tones" that are inherently generated by the amplifier. All of the harmonic frequencies are related by whole-number integers and are, therefore, musically related. The human ear can withstand about one percent total harmonic distortion before the sound becomes annoying.

Harmony Generation—The generation of other notes at musically interesting intervals along with notes. This is what a *harmonizer* does.

Headroom—The reserve power needed for peaks. It is common to use an amp capable of producing twice the power that you will need. A high-quality sound system should have 10 dB of headroom—10 dB is equal to 10 times the power.

Horizontal Deflection Plates—A pair of parallel electrodes in a CRT that moves the electron beam from side to side.

Impedance Matching—The property of resisting or controlling the current flow. Impedance matching refers to having identical impedances at the output and the input of the connecting devices, matching source and load impedances. A piece of equipment with an output impedance of 600 ohms needs to operate into an amplifier with an input impedance of at least 600 ohms. If this is not followed, excessive distortion can occur.

Indirectly-Heated Cathode—The same as a directly-heated cathode with one exception: The hot filament raises the temperature of the sleeve around the filament, and the sleeve then becomes the electron emitter.

Infinite Limiting—Occurs when a waveform is amplified infinitely and hard, and is symmetrically clipped, producing a rectangular output waveform that shares only the zero crossing with the input waveform. The result sounds buzzy.

Input Sensitivity—The minimum input signal strength for an amplifier to produce full RMS power. If the output of a piece of equipment is .775 V and the input sensitivity of the power amp is 1 V, there is no way that the amp can reach full power.

Interelectrode Capacitance—The capacitance between an electron tube electrode and the next electrode toward the anode.

Intermodulation—The production, in a non-linear circuit element, of frequencies corresponding to the sums and differences of the fundamentals and harmonics of two or more frequencies that are transmitted through that element.

Intermodulation Distortion—Differs from harmonic distortion in that the resulting ghost tones are not musically related. Instead of being related by whole-number multiples, the notes produced are sums and differences of the two frequencies. Intermodulation distortion is typically more annoying than harmonic distortion.

Ionization—The electrically-charged particles produced by high energy radiation, such as light or ultraviolet rays, or by the collision of particles during thermal agitation.

Ionization Point—The potential required to ionize the gas of a gas-filled tube. This is sometimes called the *firing point.*

Lighthouse Tube—An electron tube shaped like a lighthouse, and designed to handle large amounts of power at UHF frequencies.

Linear—Having an output that varies in direct proportion to the input.

Maximum Peak Plate Current—The highest peak current that the plate of a vacuum tube can safely pass in the direction in which the tube is designed to conduct the current.

Multi-Electrode Tube—An electron tube that contains more than three grids.

Multi-Unit Tube—An electron tube containing two or more units within the same envelope. The tube is capable of operating as a single-unit tube or as separate tubes.

Noise Addition—Noise, hiss, rumble, etc. that are deliberately added to the input signal. If noise addition is done with restraint and it matches the input signal, it can add a "breath" effect that sounds like the hiss of air when a flute is played.

Noise Gating—Modulates the output off when the input level is below a threshold. The modulation may be a square wave, or a variation of expansion where the low-level inputs are expanded down into silence, which gives a less abrupt transition.

Nonlinear—Having an output that does not rise or fall directly with the input.

Ohm's Law— The set of mathematical relationships that tie together the various characteristics of electricity. The potential power or voltage (expressed in volts ["V"] or as "E" in formulas) divided by the resistance (expressed in ohms or as "R" in formulas), is equal to the amperage or current (expressed in amps ["A"] or as "I" in formulas).

Oilcan Tube—A type of planar tube, similar to the lighthouse tube, which has cooling fins. The oilcan tube is designed to handle large amounts of power at UHF frequencies.

Parallel Connections—Occurs when one hooks up speakers to an amplifier with all of the positives to the positives and all of the negatives to the negatives. The load placed on the amplifier is increased with each additional speaker.

Peak Current—The maximum current that flows during a complete cycle.

Peak Forward Anode Voltage—The maximum instantaneous voltage appearing across the anode and the cathode in the direction in which the tube was designed to conduct current.

Peak Inverse Anode Voltage—The maximum instantaneous voltage appearing across an anode and cathode in the direction opposite to that in which the tube is designed to conduct current.

Peak Reverse Voltage—The peak AC voltage that a rectifier tube can withstand in the reverse direction.

Peak Voltage—The maximum value present in a varying or alternating voltage. This may be positive or negative.

Pentode Tube—A five-electrode electron tube containing a plate, a cathode, a control grid, and two grids.

Persistence—The duration of time for which a display remains on the face of a CRT.

Phase—When two waveforms occur at the same time, they interact with one another and create a new wave form. Phase refers to the effect one wave has on another. Two waves, which are started simultaneously and have the same amplitude and frequency, will produce a new wave with the same frequency but with greater amplitude. The amplitude will be the sum of the amplitudes of each wave; these two waves are said to be *in phase*.

Phase Distortion—Results when the phase relation of the frequency components in the output differs from the phase relation of the frequency components in the input.

Phase Inverter—An amplifier whose purpose is to shift the phase of an incoming signal voltage by 180 degrees to provide a driving voltage in combination with the original signal for a push-pull amplifier.

Phase-Lock Tracking—An electronic circuit called a *phase-locked loop* can produce an output signal that is exactly an integer multiple or small-numbers fractions of a reference signal in frequency. You can generate a signal that follows your notes.

Phase Shifting—A filter response generated by using long phase delays and mixing with the original signal to cause a number of deep notches and/or peaks in the overall filter response. This mimics the larger number of notches and peaks caused by true time-delayed flanging. This may incorporate feedback to sharpen the effect of the notches.

Phosphor—The material used to convert the energy of electrons into visible light.

Planar Tubes—An electron tube, constructed with parallel electrodes and a ceramic envelope, which is used at UHF frequencies. It is commonly referred to as a *lighthouse tube.*

Plate Dissipation—The amount of power lost as heat in the plate of a vacuum tube.

Plate Resistance—The plate voltage change divided by the resultant plate current change in a vacuum tube, all other conditions being fixed.

Power—Specifies how fast work is done, or how fast energy is transferred. Since the unit of measurement for electrical power is the watt designated with the letter "P," the formula in electrical terms is "watts = voltage x current," or "P = E x I." Wattage here is defined as the measurement of work done or energy expended.

Power Amplifier—An amplifier whose primary purpose is to deliver power into a load circuit.

Power-Handling Capacity—Refers to how much power a speaker can handle without damage. Power handling can be determined by the two most common ratings: *program* and *continuous*. Continuous (RMS) refers to a pure sine wave driving a speaker. Program power (peak) is a signal that is constantly changing, like recorded music. The program power rating is usually twice the continuous power because recorded music will reach peaks that the speaker can handle for short periods of time. Continuous sine waves make the speakers work continuously and will cause them to burn out faster.

Power Output—The AC power developed in an external, non-inductive resistor of rated value connected in the plate circuit of an amplifier. The maximum power output is limited by an arbitrary criterion of permissible total harmonic distortion.

Power Supply—A unit that supplies electrical power to another unit. It changes AC to DC and maintains a constant voltage, within limits.

Push-Pull Amplifier—Two similar amplifiers so arranged that the output voltage of one is 180 degrees out of phase with the other. Push-pull amplifiers are characterized by increased power output for a given total harmonic distortion, as this type of connection cancels the even harmonics.

Quiescence—The operating condition of a circuit when no input signal is being applied to it.

Rectifier—A device that converts alternating current (AC) to pulsating direct current (DC).

Regulator—The section in a basic power supply that maintains the output of the power supply at a constant level in spite of large changes in load current or input line voltage.

Remote Cutoff Tube—An electron tube in which the control grid wires are farther apart at the centers than at the ends. This arrangement allows the tube to amplify large signals without being driven into cutoff. This is also called a *variable mu tube*.

Resistance—The internal friction involved in the passage of electrons through a wire or any other material. In order to use electricity, you must be able to control the flow of current—this is done with resistance. The degree of resistance is measured in ohms; another term used for resistance is *impedance*. A speaker is a type of resistor, which is why a speaker's input is described as ohms.

Resonance—A filter with a boost frequency at a narrow range of frequencies. It sounds like a wah pedal when the pedal is not being moved.

Reverberation—The tendency for sound to continue after the original sound has ceased. It is caused by sound waves bouncing around a room and hitting the ear at slightly different intervals.

RGK—The symbol used to express the resistance between the grid and the cathode of an electron tube.

Ripple Frequency—The frequency of a ripple current. In a full wave rectifier, it is twice the input line frequency.

Ripple Voltage—The alternating component of unidirectional voltage. This component is small compared to the direct component.

RPK—The symbol used to represent the variable resistance between the cathode and the plate of a tube.

Saturation—The point at which a further increase in plate voltage no longer produces an increase in plate current in a tube. At this point, the upper limit of the conduction capabilities of a tube has been reached.

Screen Grid—A grid placed between the control grid and the plate in a tube; it is usually maintained at a positive potential.

Secondary Emission—The liberation of electrons from an element, other than the cathode, as a result of being struck by other high velocity electrons.

Self-Bias—The voltage developed by the flow of vacuum tube current through a resistor in a grid or cathode lead.

Sensitivity—Most manufacturers publish a specification called sensitivity (*sound pressure level* or *SPL*). This is a test performed by sending a swept sine wave or pink noise through the speaker at one watt of power. An SPL meter is held one meter away and a reading is obtained. A speaker with a rating of 106 dB will be louder than a speaker of 103 dB (remember the "3 dB = double the power" rule).

Series Connection—A wiring situation where signal runs in line from one item to the next. A good example of series connections are the Christmas tree lights you may use or have seen—when one goes out, they all go out because the signal or voltage runs in line from one to the other. To calculate the total impedance of a series connection, add the individual load impedances together. Two 4-ohm speakers in series form an 8-ohm load.

Series Parallel—Series parallel connections allow sub-grouping of speakers in order to achieve any needed load impedance. To calculate the total impedance, group all of the series connection together and add the impedances of each speaker within each series group. Treat each series group as a single value and connect all of the series groups in parallel. As a general rule, if you were, for example, wiring a four-twelve cabinet, if each speaker was 8 ohms, then the overall impedance would be 8 ohms.

Sharp Cutoff Tube Bias—The opposite of remote cutoff. In an electron tube that has evenly spaced grid wires, the amplification of the sharp cutoff tube is limited by the bias voltage and characteristics.

Space Charge—An electrical charge distributed throughout a volume or space.

Symmetrical Clipping—On a sine wave, the tops and bottoms of a waveform are clipped at equal amounts. Although this is a simplistic explanation for a simple sine wave, symmetrical clipping generates only odd-order harmonics, giving a raspy or distorted sound to a waveform. The hardness or softness of the clipping matters. *Hard clipping* results when the output wave stays at the clipping level until the input drops below the clipping level again, giving flat tops and bottoms to the clipped output. Hard clipping emphasizes the higher-order harmonics (7th and up). *Soft clipping* has no abrupt clipping level, but gently rounds the top and bottom of the output waveform. Soft clipping emphasizes the lower-order harmonics (3rd and 5th).

Talk Box—An effect created by using an amplifier connected to a high-frequency horn driver to produce sound that is conducted into your mouth by a tube. You can then use the resonances of your mouth to shape the instrument sound (e.g., mouth the words to a song), which is picked up by a microphone.

Tetrode Tube—A four-electrode electron tube containing a plate, a cathode, a control grid, and a screen grid.

Thermionic Emission—Emission of electrons from a solid body as a result of elevated temperature.

Thyratron Tube—A gas-filled triode in which a sufficiently large positive pulse applied to the control grid ionizes the gas and causes the tube to conduct, after which the control grid has no effect in conduction.

Transconductance—A measure of the change in plate current to a change in grid voltage with the plate voltage held constant. Transconductance (g_m) is usually expressed in micro ohms or milliohms, and is the ratio of a small change in the magnitude of the alternating currents in a phase component that flows in the second electrode to a small change in the alternating voltage of the first electrodes, all other electrode voltages being constant.

Transit Time—The time an electron takes to cross the distance between a cathode and a plate.

Tremolo—The cyclical variation of volume by a low frequency oscillator; the parameters are waveforms of the LFO (low-frequency oscillator) frequency and depth of modulation. While the terms "tremolo" and "vibrato" are often used interchangeably, tremolo is defined by variations in loudness whereas vibrato is defined by variations in pitch and frequency.

Triode Tube—A three-electrode electron tube containing a plate, a cathode, and a control grid.

Tube Voltage Drop—In a vacuum tube, the tube voltage drop varies with the current, and is the anode voltage produced by a specific plate current. Tube voltage drop in a gas vapor–filled tube is the anode-to-cathode voltage during the conducting period.

Undistorted Power Output—Defined as the power output delivered by a vacuum tube into a resistance load, under the conditions that the total generated harmonic distortion with a sinusoidal excitation voltage shall not exceed an arbitrary criterion of permissible total harmonic distortion of five percent.

Vertical Deflection Plates—A pair of parallel electrodes in a CRT that move the electron beam up and down.

Vibrato—A cyclical variation in the basic frequency of the input signal, similar to the effect of a whammy bar on a guitar. A true vibrato as an effect requires a time delay circuit. Vibrato is defined by variations in pitch and frequency.

Voltage Amplifier—An amplifier whose primary purpose is to obtain a voltage gain without regard to the power delivered into its output circuit.

Voltage Gain—Ratio of voltage across a specified load. It is the ratio of voltage developed across the plate impedance to the exciting grid voltage.

Wah—A resonator whose center frequency can be moved up and down by the use of a pedal. The "wah" name comes from the way it mimics the moving resonance of human speech as the sound "wah" is made.

SELECTIVE INDEX

A

active splitter, 48, 50
amplifier modification, 57–103

B

beam power tube, 19, 22, 137
biasing, 81–84, 137
buffer, 48–51, 66

C

cathode, 19–22, 137
cathode biasing, 81
chemicals, 13–14
chiller, 13
Class A amplifier, 77–78, 138
Class AB amplifier, 77–78, 138
Class B amplifier, 78, 138
common cathode, 58–59, 73
Concertina splitter, 72
control grid, 20–22, 137, 139, 144–148
Corona Dope, 14

D

decoupled supplies, 92
de Forrest, Lee, 23–24
DeoxIT, 14
differential splitter, 73
distortion generator, 57, 86–87
dummy load, 11

E

effects loop, 55, 57, 66–67, 92, 98, 100–101

F

feedback circuit, 80–81
Fender, Leo, 57
Fender date code, 46
FET, 36, 97, 102
filament, 13, 19–21, 23, 95–96, 138, 140–142
fixed bias, 81–83, 141
foldback reverb, 69
footswitch, 98, 100–103